# From the: CREATOR

## Back from the grave...

This makes two years of Stiff Magazine! Many said we would fail within the first year, but here we are. Not only have we survived, but we are also launching a second title very soon!

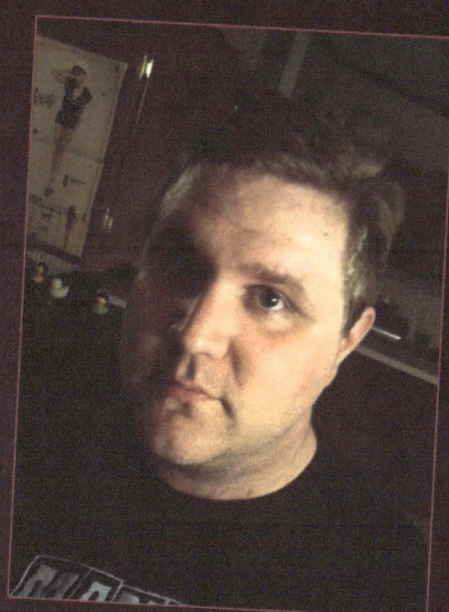

Photo: © Miss Envy

We have been hard at work for the last several months, looking at what else we could offer you guys, and found out we just couldn't fit everything in this magazine. We even tried holding content over for another issue, which just made the next one have excess content. The big question was what should we do? I hate throwing things out that someone put real effort into, so we have decided to offer a second magazine, for free.

We expect the first offering of this new title to become available in November, and it will be going out as an e-magazine. Think of it as a stripped down Stiffmag aimed at a mobile community of readers.

This also presents us with a new option for models. We can now accept third party submissions with the new magazine! I know many of you are interested in working with us, but traveling to us isn't always possible. Now there's a solution.

Finally, I'd like to salute those of you that said we would fail. Please feel free to tell me how many issues I have left. We have surpassed your expectations, and I offer you a well-valued life lesson. I don't do this for the money or the glory. I do this because I enjoy it. I've survived at independent publishing since 1998 in various forms, and I'm here to stay.

That said, many thanks to all of you for your continued support. Oh yes...

## HAPPY HALLOWEEN!

~Shane of the Dead

Questions? Comments? Suggestions? Drop me a line at: admin@graveyardgirls.net

# ON THE INSIDE

ON THE COVER: *"Leigh Fox"* by Mystic

## INSIDE:

## STAFF:

• Shane of the Dead - Creator/Publisher GraveyardGirls.net
• Dave Harlequin - Editor in Chief GraveyardGirls.net
• Mystic - Creative Dir./Photographer in Chief TheArtOfMystic.com

• Justin Kates - Stiff Photographer TheJustinKates.com
• Immortal Image - Stiff Photographer immortalimagephoto.com
• Billy Liner - Stiff Photographer at Large modelmayhem.com/linerb

• Dave Ward - Operations Assistant GraveyardGirls.net
• Hollie Quinn - Event Merchandise GraveyardGirls.net
• James Nimmons - Promotions/Regional Sales GraveyardGirls.net

## CONTRIBUTING WRITERS

• Andrea Albin
• Anthony Corona
• Antigone Kilma
• Coty Keziah
• Dave Mongeni
• Dii Raine
• Epic Nguyen
• Rabbi Ben Thorstein
• Rich Sigfrit
• Whitley Albury

## REGISTER@STIFFMAG.COM

Stiff Mag™ presented by GraveyardGirls Publishing Group

# STIFF
## FROM THE EDITOR

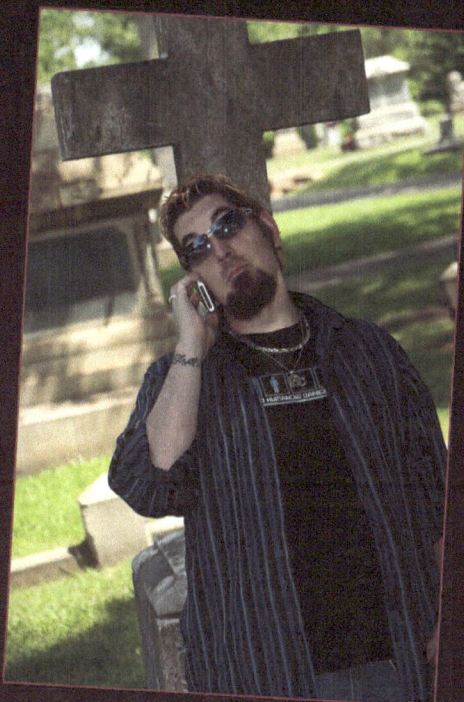

## GREETINGS FELLOW STIFFS!

Well folks, we did it, year two is officially in the books! It hasn't always been easy, but thanks to the continued support of our staff, sponsors and readers, we're still going strong! I'm sure there were a lot of people out there who didn't think we'd make it this far, and it's with that in mind that I very proudly say…

## Welcome to Issue #8 of Stiff Magazine!

Since the last issue, we've been hard at work on so many fronts, including getting the next edition of our "After Dark" series completed, preparing to launch a brand new 2nd magazine title, and of course, gearing up for the super-busy Fall events season! We've already kicked things off back in September at our home club of Ground Zero in Spartanburg SC with the Graveyard Girls Whiskey Doubleshot party, and made our return to the Charlotte-area for the 2011 Modern Film Fest, where we also took part in their annual Idiot Circle Zombie Walk. Next up, we're making a trip down to Columbia SC for RoundCon 2011 where we'll be featured guests, and will be hosting tons of really cool horror programming and special events. After that, we'll be headed up to Salisbury NC for our 4th Annual Miss Nightmerica Pageant, where we'll be giving away tons of cash/prizes along with crowning this year's hottest ghoul. But that's not even close to everything we've got going on this season! Be sure to check our events listing in this issue, and if you haven't already, please like us on Facebook at facebook.com/STIFFmag for more event info and frequent updates on everything we've got going on here at the graveyard!

In this issue, we've got plenty of drop-dead gorgeous models and exclusive content for your viewing pleasure, including a very special interview with the original Jason Voorhees and tons of other cool stuff for the expanded Halloween Edition! Many thanks to everyone who contributed to getting issue #8 off the ground, all of our wonderful sponsors, and of course, to all of you readers… we wouldn't be here without you!

Happy Halloween from all of us here at Stiff Magazine!

Cheers!
Dave Harlequin - Editor in Chief

Questions? Comments? Suggestions? Drop me a line at: dave@graveyardgirls.net

## PART 4: "Problems and Complications: Don't Panic!"
by: Dii Raine

In this final installment, I will touch (very briefly) on a few common complications that you may experience during your new piercing's healing process. For a more extensive look at complications, what causes them, and what can be done to remedy them, check out Elayne Angel's "The Piercing Bible: The Definitive Guide to Safe Body Piercing".

My words of wisdom for this issue are simple… it is probably not an infection, and you are not dying. Chances are, what you think is a raging infection is a minor, common complication that sometimes plagues a healing piercing. Complications can be caused by jewelry that is too tight due to improper piercing or excessive swelling; minor tears caused by jewelry getting caught on clothes, blankets, towels, etc; poor quality jewelry; and several other factors. The first thing to remember when a complication arises with a piercing is to not panic. The second is to seek advice from your piercer (not your friends/family) immediately.

Occasionally, you may notice a small bump next to or on your piercing. This lump of skin may be a solid mass of skin, or it may be filled with white or yellow discharge.  Before you lose your cool and start planning your funeral, think to yourself: "has someone or something recently yanked or pulled on my piercing?" Chances are, this nasty little lump is a keloid, or hypertrophic scarring caused by trauma to the healing piercing. Do not remove the jewelry from the piercing. Removing your jewelry will not make this problem go away, and removing the jewelry from the tract will prevent drainage that is essential to healing. Contact your piercer and he/she will work with you to remedy this problem. The solution may be as simple as a few warm compresses with saline or a tea bag, or may be as extensive as a series of different remedies, depending on your unique case. Keep in mind that a clear, white, or yellow discharge is normal during the healing process. This is a byproduct of your skin cells rebuilding themselves. This is also what causes the hard, dry "crusties" you will notice accumulating on your jewelry.

Another complication that sometimes arises with a piercing is one that piercees tend to bring upon themselves: skin irritation resulting from cheap jewelry. Your piercer doesn't advise you to stay away from cheap and inexpensive jewelry just to fatten his/her wallet. Body piercers advise against jewelry from your local cheap-o super center, the hottest mall store, flea markets, yard sales, and head shops (just to name a few places) because the quality of jewelry can drastically affect the health of a piercing. Cheap jewelry material can be harmful and irritating…

especially to a new piercing. Professional body piercers take great care to ensure that you are offered only the highest quality jewelry. Cheap alternatives you find in strip malls and flea markets are often bought in bulk, not checked for imperfections, made of inferior materials, and are often left in bins and displays for people to sift through with dirty hands. That ninety-nine cent navel jewelry from the bargain bin could cost you hundreds of dollars in doctor's bills in the long run.

Keep in mind that although it is your piercer's responsibility to provide a clean, safe, sterile environment for you to be pierced in, it is your responsibility to follow the aftercare and professional advice you are given. Also keep in mind that although complications can be caused by outside sources, sometimes things just happen. Everyone's body reacts differently to piercings and occasionally; a certain piercing may not be what's right for you.

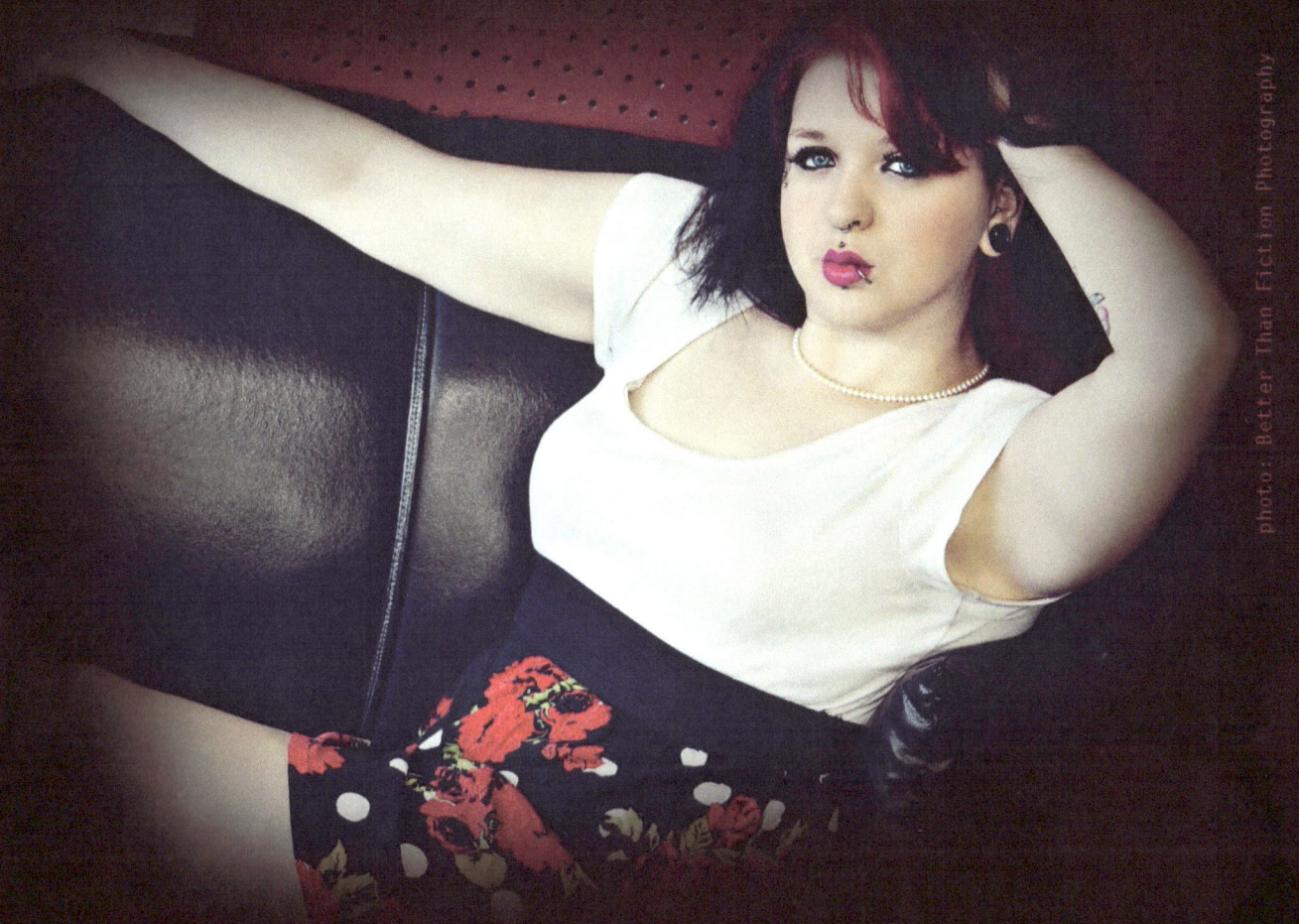

photo: Better Than Fiction Photography

*(Dii has been a body piercer for over 3 years at Iron|Ink Tattoos and Piercing in Bostic, NC. She would like to extend a special thanks to Cindy Martin and SunShine McCurry for their help with this article. Please Note: the personal views & professional opinions expressed by Dii are not necessarily those of Stiff Magazine or Graveyard Girls Entertainment- so if she, or any other columnist pisses you off, don't sue us!)*

# GRAVEYARDGIRL: XLCR MOON

The lovely Xlcr Moon spends much of her time traveling around the United States for shoots, but currently resides in Dallas, Texas. Her modeling experience began with her first shoot in 2005. She tells us *"I love a challenge and enjoy being different characters for each shoot."*

Her musical tastes *"anything but country and rap,"* and she also adds with much exclamation *"I hate country!!"* As for bands she does listen to, favorite bands include *"Type O Negative, A Perfect Circle, Static X, old Alice n Chains, Chevelle, Korn, Prodigy, Taproot, Trapt, Incubus... I could go on forever."*

In regard to film interests she says, *"I love horror movies and good comedies, but I also enjoy a good action packed film, and horror movies that have a lot of action and sarcasm are absolutely my fave!"*

You'll fit right in around here Xlcr... Welcome to the family!

STUDIOS

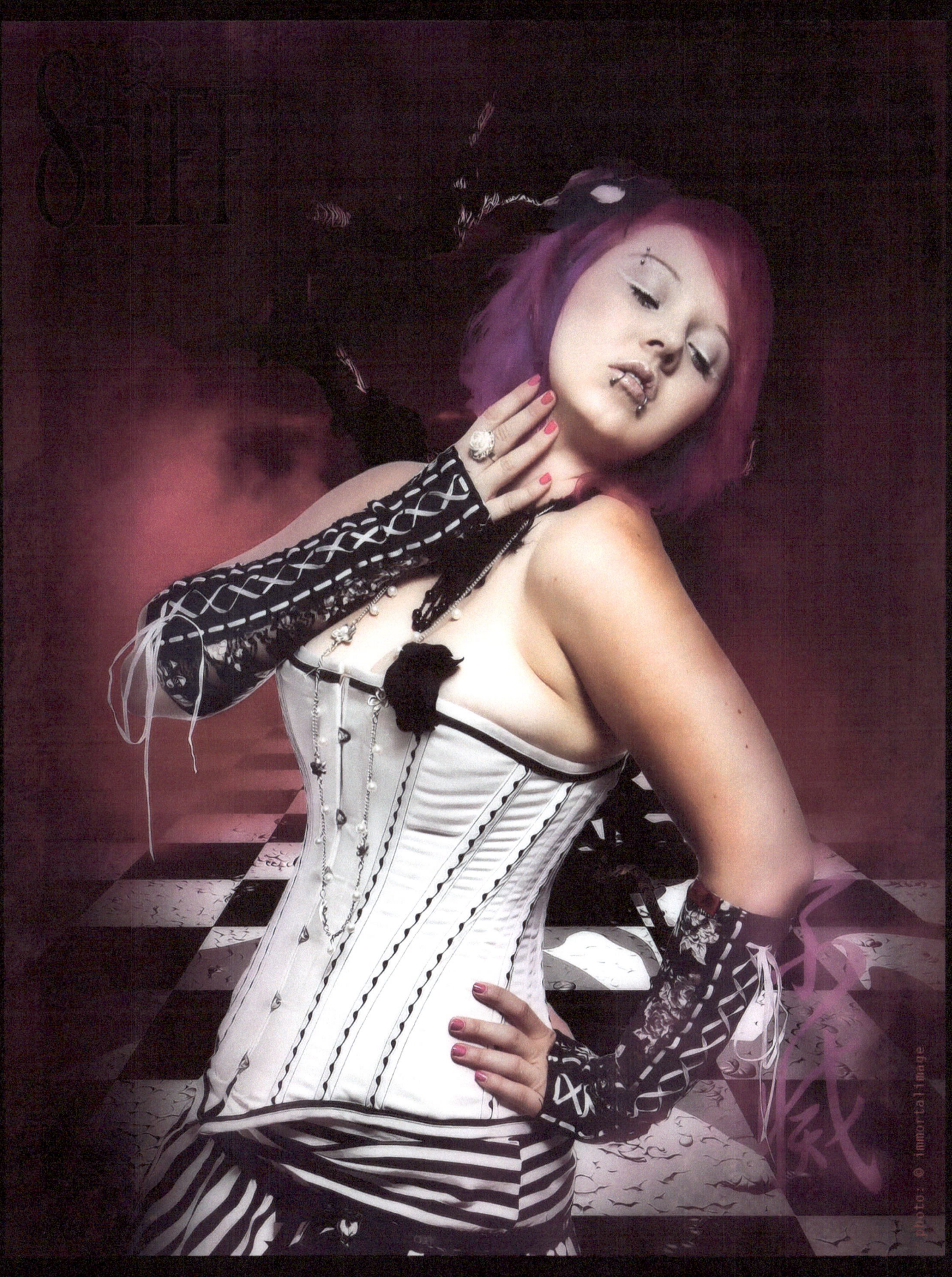

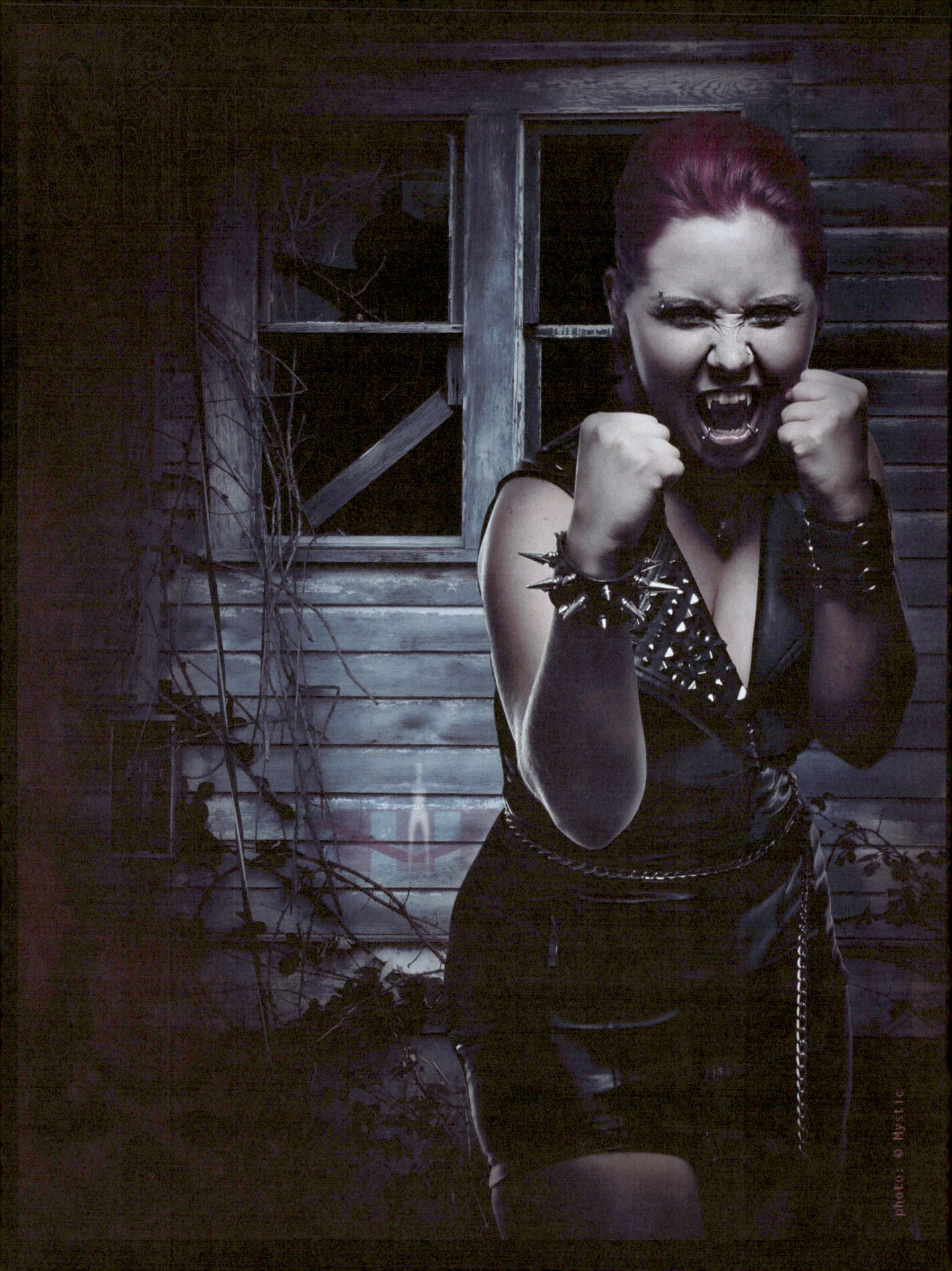

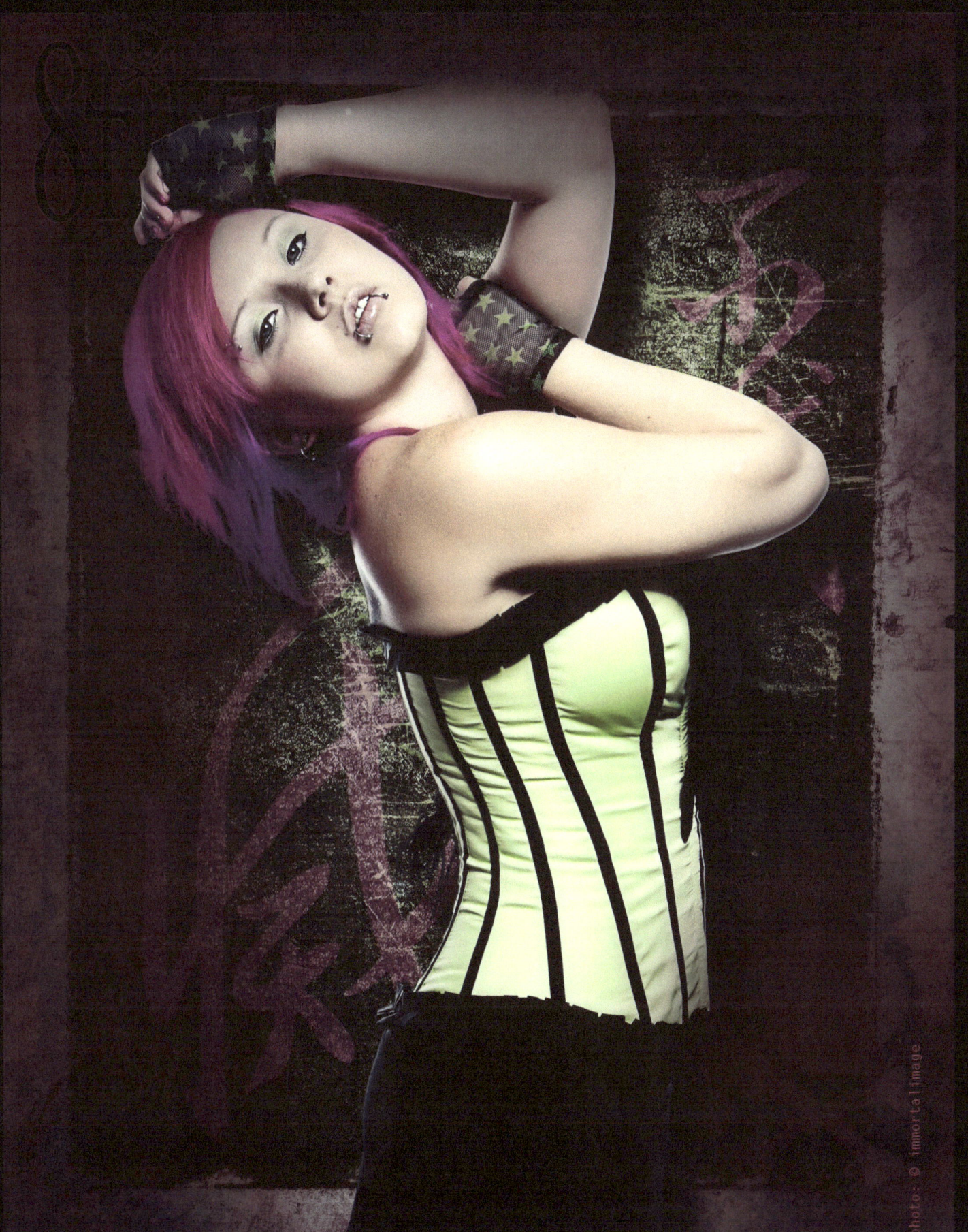

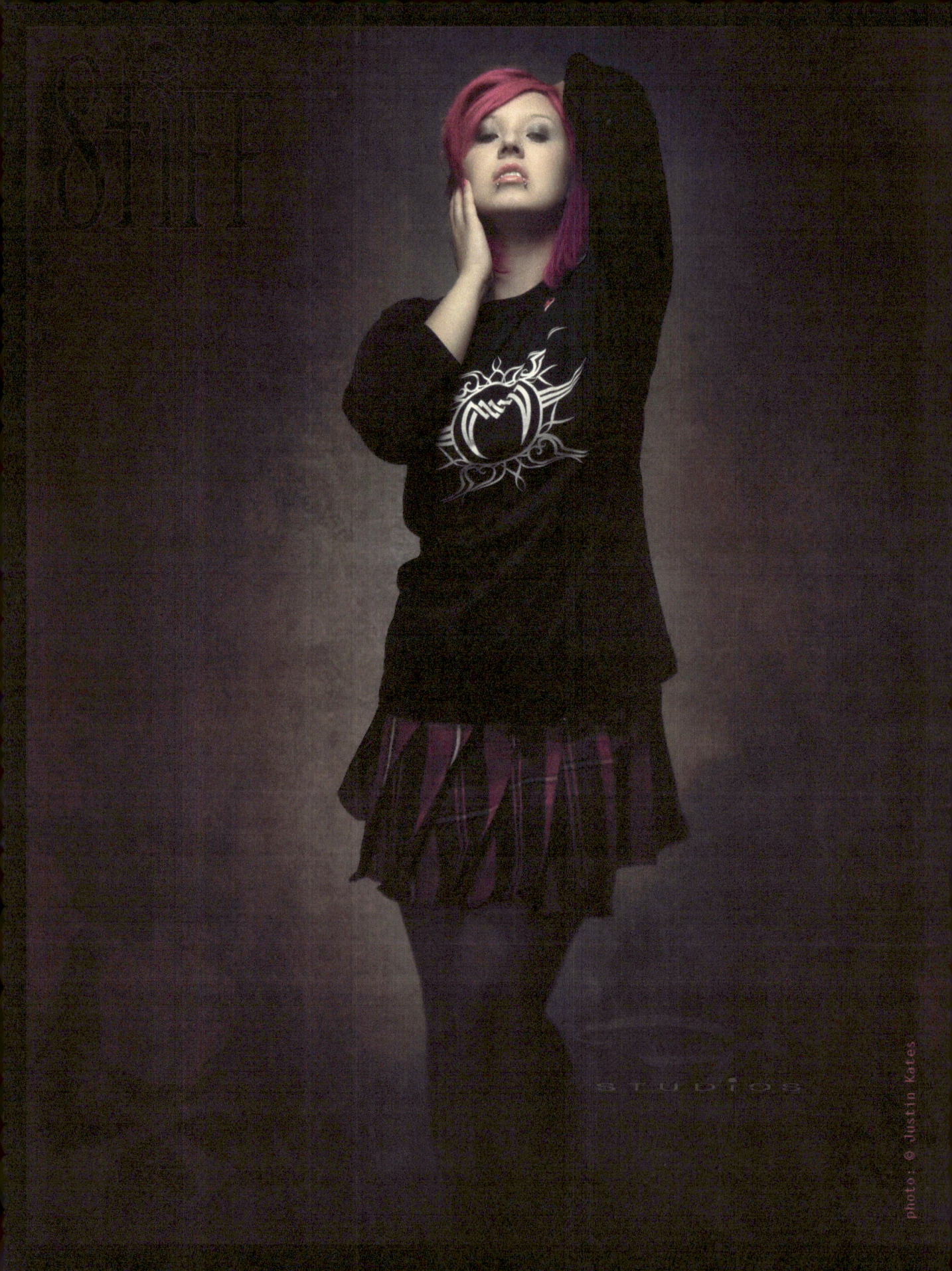

STIFF

STUDIOS

photo: © Justin Kates

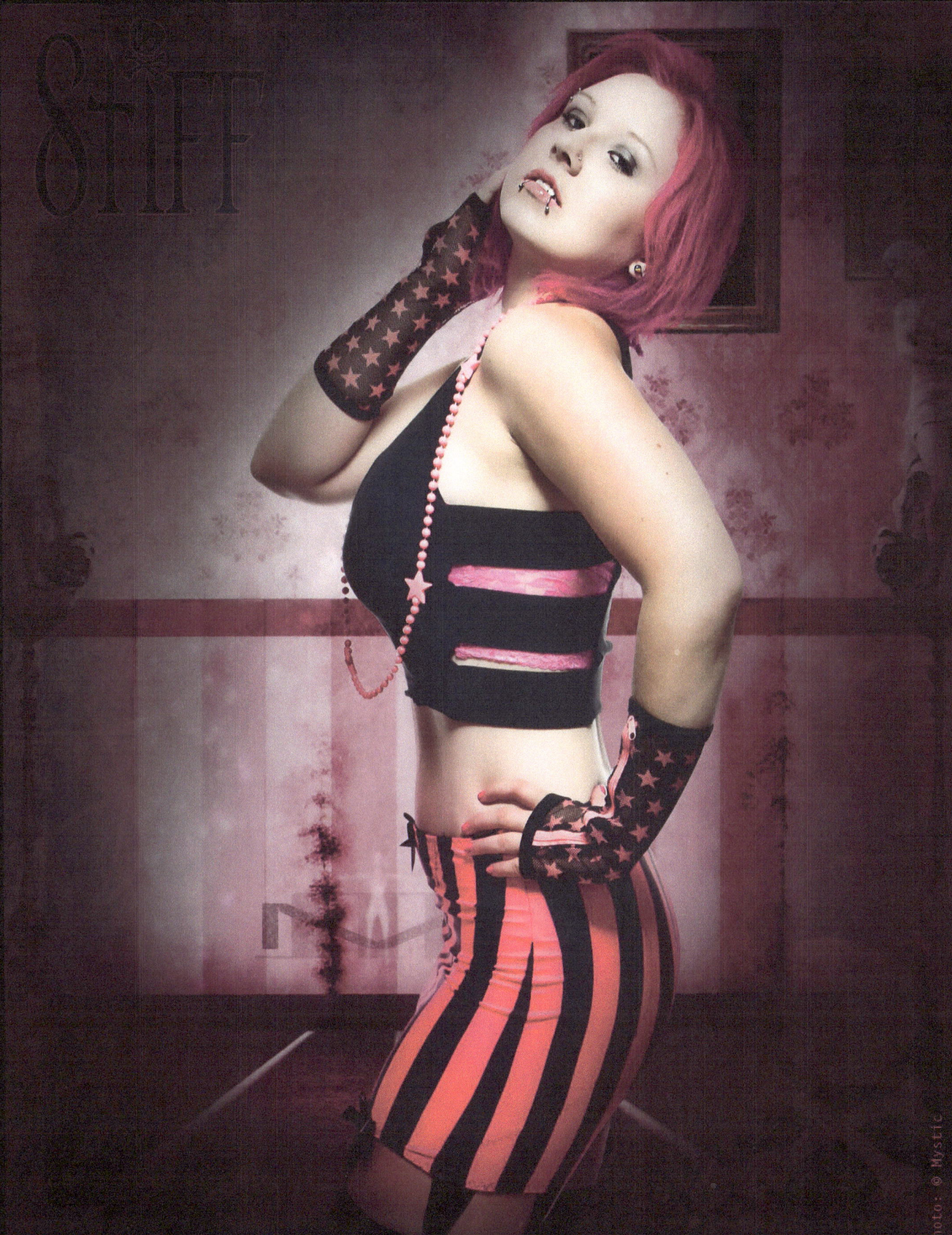

STiFF

Reviews: **MUSIC**

Featured Band:
Midnight Syndicate: "Carnival Arcane"
by: Anthony Corona

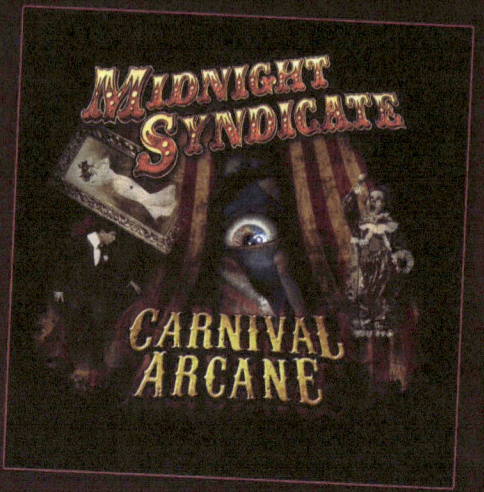

While the name Midnight Syndicate may not be
instantly-recognized with the larger public, their
music is inescapable. One would need to shelter
themselves entirely from both horror movies; video
games and Halloween alike in order to completely
avoid the group. After their first release in 1998
the band has released over 14 albums, the music for
which has been licensed for both the soundtracks and
scores for countless movies, TV shows, video games
as well as a few other songs. In 2003 the band even
produced the first official soundtrack score for
the legendary "Dungeons & Dragons" roleplaying game.

Now with Halloween approaching us in 2011, fans and anyone looking to make a
Haunted Attraction should look for Midnight Syndicate's latest release, "Carnival
Arcane." Make no mistake; Midnight Syndicate makes the perfect soundtrack for
haunted houses and they're very aware of this. With no small amount of whimsy,
composer Edward Douglas refers to their work as "imaginary soundtracks," and
claims "the new album feels more like a movie than anything we've done to date."
Each album is designed to help the reader build a story to accompany the music.
Out of 25 tracks on this latest effort, anyone could easily cherry pick the songs
that best fit their own ideas for their own haunted house.

It would have been easy for a band making a carnival-themed album to focus on the
traditional "Hurdy-Gurdy" machines and music to create their album. However doing
that would limit their audience, most people who would purchase their albums need
it for a specific haunted house, and while they can always look to the group's
earlier albums the band simply wasn't lazy enough to let it be. Borrowing from
the music and referencing the actual history of the late 19th Century and early
20th Century, "Carnival Arcane" is a sepia-toned orchestral jack-of-all-trades,
reserving the bulk of the hurdy-gurdy organs and oppressive clown laughter for
the last few tracks. Naturally perfect for a creepy or haunted carnival, but more
than a few of the songs could fit among other settings just as well. "Strange
Menagerie" is a sweeping, epic piece just as fitting in a medieval or more open
setting, and "Agent of Fortune" is slow and creepy, its crescendos betraying
little of its carnival roots and leaving it suitable for anyone's own creepy
needs. "Pulling the Strings" and its orchestral themes, may make listeners feel
familiar and even remind them of some of the more popular Japanese RPG's.

Ultimately, Midnight Syndicate's work is simultaneously unique and familiar. No band does what they do independently. Where some composers and groups make scores for individual films, Midnight Syndicate seemingly lacks the patience for this, opting instead to make the soundtrack and wait for the films to come. Like most scores however, only the most adamant listeners will enjoy the music on their own or in their spare time. Rather, Midnight Syndicate finds its home in your home, backyard, or wherever you've set up a sound system along with traps, lights, curtains and fog machines to scare the crap out of the neighborhood kids. This is where it belongs, ultimately Midnight Syndicate's music is whatever the listener makes of it, and there is simply no better place for it.

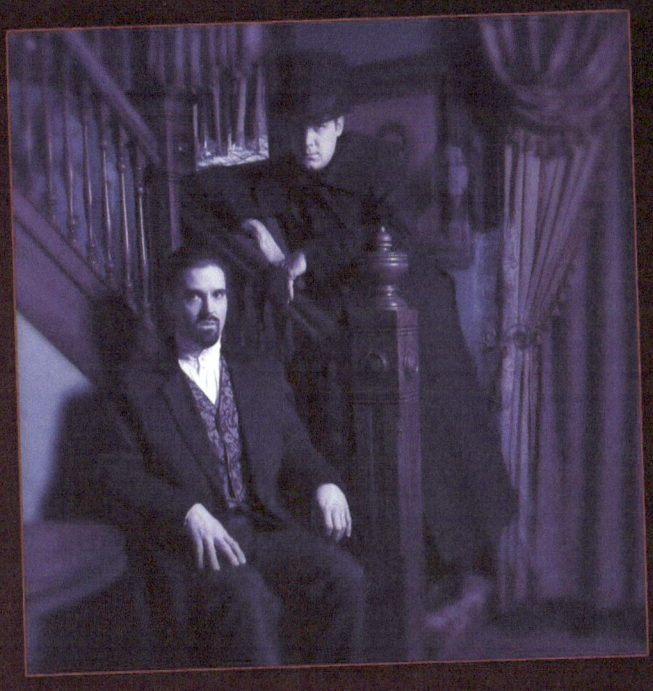

Photos Courtesy of: Linfaldia Records (BMI)

www.midnightsyndicate.com

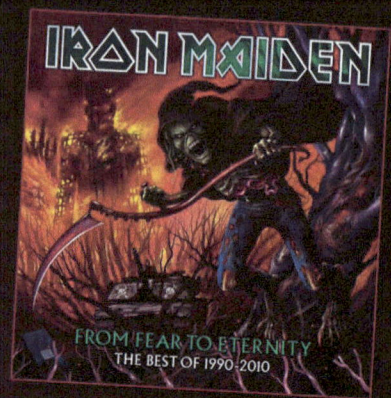

## Iron Maiden: "From Fear To Eternity"
by: Whitley Albury

The forefathers of metal, Iron Maiden, have released their seventh best-of two-disc package: "From Fear To Eternity: The Best of 1990-2010." This new album is a 23 track follow up to 2008's "Back In Time," featuring songs from the last twenty years left off of the other six greatest hits efforts. Among the tracks are four that were originally recorded by Blaze Bayley, who fronted the band from 1994 until 1999, but were re-recorded live with Bruce Dickinson on vocals.

If you're a hardcore Maiden fan, and/or have the other six greatest hits albums, I'd go ahead and suggest getting this one too. But if you have their complete discography already, I'd say just get the live tracks online if you really want them.                www.ironmaiden.com

## The Birthday Massacre: "Imaginary Monsters"
by: Dave Harlequin

Canadian synth-rockers The Birthday Massacre return with their latest EP: "Imaginary Monsters," out now on Metropolis Records. Less than a year after the release of their highly successful LP "Pins and Needles," the new eight-track EP features three brand-new songs, and five remixes of songs from their previous release.

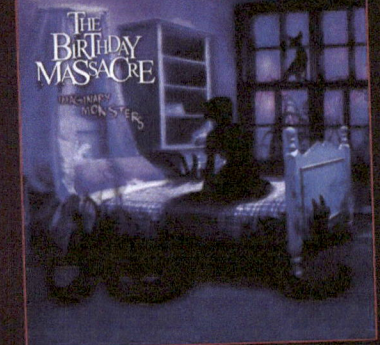

The album leads off with the three new tracks, which were likely cut from the final tracklist of their previous album. Whatever that reason may have been, it certainly wasn't for lack of quality; the new songs have the same high-quality production and signature dark-fantasy, atmospheric elements blended with 80's-esque synthpop that their fans love about them. The album then proceeds into various remixes of TBM songs from some of the biggest names in EBM and industrial music, including Assemblage 23, Combichrist, and Tim Skold. While the remixes aren't necessarily bad, they're also nothing particularly special, and are truly outshined by the new material the record opened with.

Also of note, the new EP comes with a bonus of the official music video of "In The Dark," which really showcases the band's incredible talents as visual artists. The video is excellently produced, visually striking, and deliciously macabre, paying homage to various iconic horror films, while maintaining the visual elements the band is known for.

Overall, "Imaginary Monsters" is a very respectable addition to the band's already impressive resume, which is sure to keep their fans happy and even win them some new ones in the process. Unlike a typical remix EP, this one is definitely worth picking up for the new songs, and especially the new video. Highly recommended.          www.thebirthdaymassacre.com

# Theatre Of Tragedy: "Last Curtain Call"
by: Whitley Albury

Norwegian industrial-rock giants Theatre of Tragedy's latest (and alleged final) album, "Last Curtain Call", is a live CD/DVD combo recorded at their last concert at Folken, Stavanger, Norway. The "Repo: The Genetic Opera-Meets-Rammstein" sound is very melodic and piano laden, but Nell Sigland's operatic vocals soar high above the dark, heavy guitars. Raymond István Rohonyi's deep growls juxtaposed against Sigland's soprano almost give the listener a sense of an angel and demon being in the same band. For a first-time listener like myself, it takes a little while to adjust to it after listening to metal and punk for years, but once adjusted, I truly enjoyed listening.

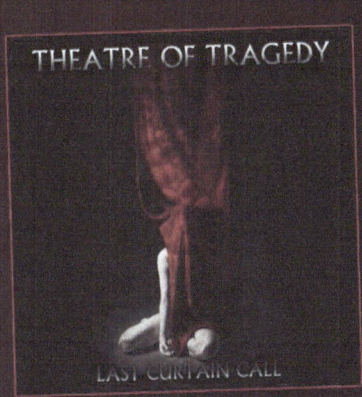

The new album features ten live tracks on the CD while the DVD has eighteen live videos. In addition, the DVD also features three documentaries: "The Last Tour", "The Last Rehearsal", and exclusive interviews with the band. Overall, "Last Curtain Call" is a very respectable collection and behind the scenes look at a great band. For diehard Theatre of Tragedy fans, this one is a must-have.              www.theatreoftragedy.com

# Cold: "SuperFiction"
by: Whitley Albury

Jacksonville, Florida rockers Cold return with "SuperFiction", their first album in six years. Since their three-year hiatus, Cold has taken their direction into more of an artistic one, as the title of the new album suggests. Each song even has its own piece of artwork that goes with it.  Upon first listen, the tracks all seem to blur together, except for "American Dream", which, to me, is the standout track. According to lead vocalist Scooter Ward, while the album may still be dark, the band felt much happier recording this than any other album.

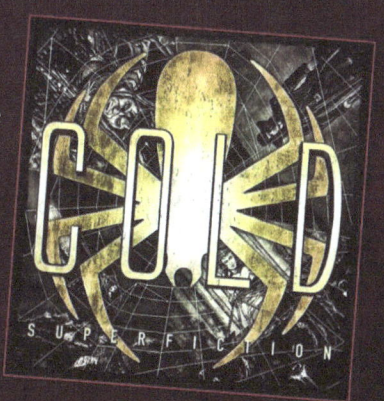

Even though it takes a listen or two to really get into the album, I think it's really quite good. It was well worth the six-year wait. Overall, "SuperFiction" isn't Cold's best work, but is still a promising sign of things to come.              www.coldarmy.com

## Lesley Pratt Bannatyne's "Halloween Nation"
by: Coty Keziah

For the longest time I believed that Halloween was this small little holiday that was only celebrated by small children and college students with too much time on their hands.  The book "Halloween Nation: Behind the Scenes of America's Fright Night" however, opened my eyes to a country obsessed with this holiday to the point of making it a one of the biggest holidays to ever be celebrated.  Upon reading this book I noticed its format, which clearly mirrors that of a textbook.  If anything, this book would be perfect for a college course on American Cultures and holiday traditions.

Lesley Pratt Bannatyne fills the reader's head with more knowledge on Halloween than I thought was physically possible.  It shows that people all over America are working hard each year to make one little night at the end of October the best night of theirs, or anyone else's life. With ten exceptionally well-written and lengthy chapters, any Halloween (or horror) fan will certainly enjoy what it has to say.

Bannatyne was anything but lazy when writing this informational piece.  Instead of internet-based or standard book research, she traveled the country in order to find the origins of each tradition that this horrific holiday had to offer.  This clearly shows that this book was written for Halloween fans by Halloween fans.  As I delved deeper into the book it became clear that this was an expertly crafted documentary on paper, only without the lost details one would expect from a film translation.  Her writing style gives so much detail about how each person reacted to her questions, or how a certain object looked, that it almost felt as if I was traveling with the author and meeting these people for myself.

The pictures in the book, however, leave much to be desired.  As much as I enjoy seeing for myself what certain costumes and makeup people have in various places around the country, sometimes they feel out of place, have been put in a page late or a page early, or really just have nothing to do with the page in general.  Also, many of the pictures are spread amongst two pages and many details of the pictures have been lost in the spine of book. I do not blame the author for this mistake, but regardless, it is a minor distraction.

Whether you are a hardcore Halloween
fanatic, or you only have a slight
interest in the holiday, like me, you will
enjoy this book.  It is filled with
in-depth descriptions of haunted houses,
the history of the zombie craze, and the
origins behind the Jack O' Lantern's eerie
grimace, and nature.  Overall, this book
is amazingly crafted and will have you
begging for more by the end of chapter 10.
I give this great book a full 5 out of 5
scars.

ISBN: 9781589806801

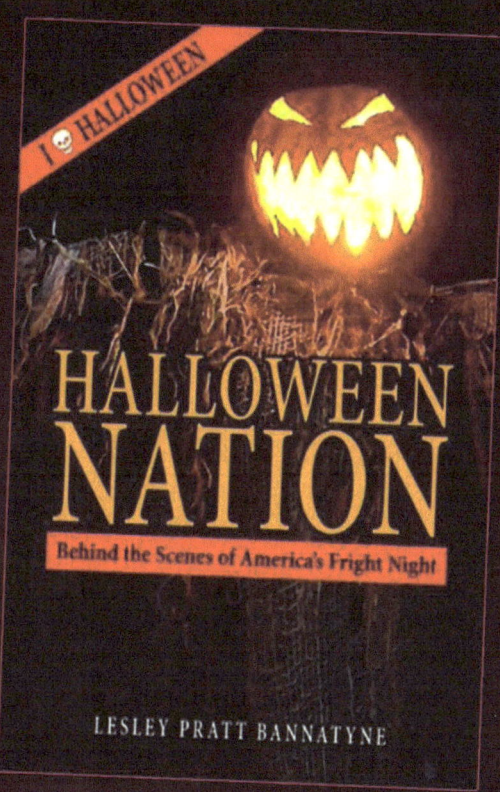

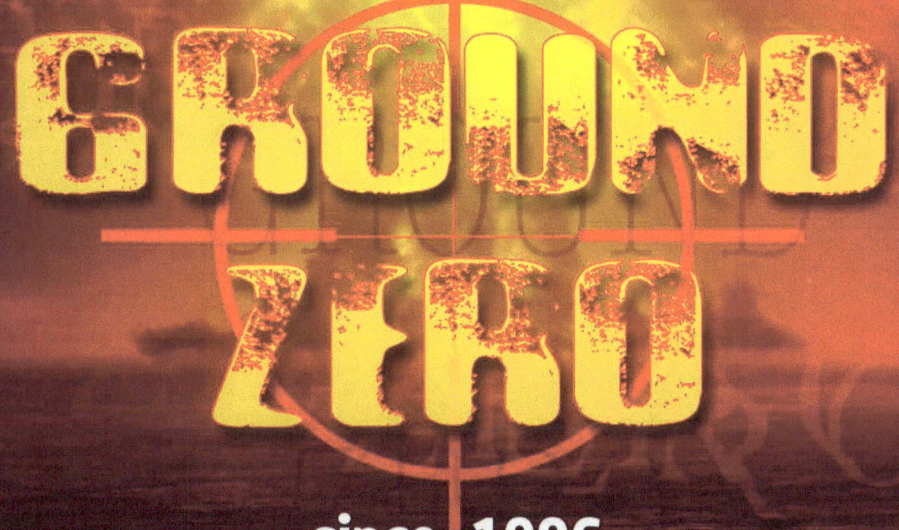

South Carolina's PREMIERE music venue

since 1996

3059 HOWARD ST. • SPARTANBURG, SC
MYSPACE.COM/GROUNDZEROROCKS  864-948-1661

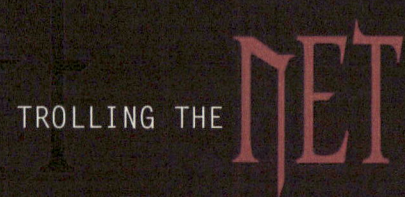

## Google+ ("Another Freakin' Social Network")
by: Podcasting's Rich Sigfrit

I'm sure after reading the title, some of you were excited that it was an announcement for a sequel to the award winning movie: "The Social Network". Nope. Although, now that you think about it, what would it be called? Perhaps "The Social Network 2: The Legend of LiveJournal Gold"? "The Return of Jaiku"? Doubtful. Sadly, that picture will only live in our imaginations, as we'll be chatting about Google+, the latest (insert most recent social zeit-geist) killer. Some of us remember the days of Myspace/LiveJournal (kids, look it up). Others recall the days where forums and chat-rooms were where we spent most of our online time. Four or five of you remember BBSes (don't forget, Matlock is coming on in an hour). But why even get into them at all, if they aren't going to last? Because, you non-conformist, all your friends are there.

Here's a quick rundown of the big three…

Facebook: 640,000,000 users. Around since: 2004. It has posts, photos, likes and ads. (Ads? Someone selling something on the Internet?) And specifically targeted ones, at that (Cialis?! Those sons of...). It also has games that post on your wall whenever it's time to harvest the corn from the spot where you buried that hobo you slaughtered.

Twitter:  175,000,000 users. Around since: 2006. It has posts but requires third party sites to post pics and ids. Comments aren't threaded and it allows for only 140 characters per post. With the majority of user posts having the content value of most Reality TV, I'm surprised it's lasted as long as it has.  Oh wait, it's because reality stars find their value by how many followers they have (I have 437!)

Google+: 25,000,000 users. Resurrected (from Google Buzz): June 2011. Still in its early adopter phase, it's just like a combination of Facebook and Twitter. (TwitBook. FaceTweeter. TwitOnMyFace?) The biggest reasons to switch to Google+ are the circles. You can place your friends into various circles and make posts and photos available to just those specific groups. Or just to ONE of the circles. Or no one but the Google+ account you set up for your iguana.

So which should you choose?  Why not all of them?  They're all totally free. Most mobile phones have apps that post to each (some apps will post to all of them). And that way, none of your exes will have to miss out on knowing every detail about your life.  You don't want to leave anyone out of your latest update proclaiming that you're at Starbucks and your Iguana just ate a purse dog. After all folks, it's the Internet… isn't it there to be trolled??? Currently, Google+ is in beta testing (so you'll have to get one of your real life and/or Facebook friends to send you an invite) but should be 100% public very soon. Check it out for yourself: http://plus.google.com Enjoy!

(Rich Sigfrit is an award-winning podcaster, writer, and voice-actor based out of Raleigh, NC. He is the host/producer of several online programs, as well as a 6-time Parsec Award Finalist, and has been featured in the book "Podcasting For Dummies." For more information on Rich Sigfrit please visit www.outcastmultimedia.com)

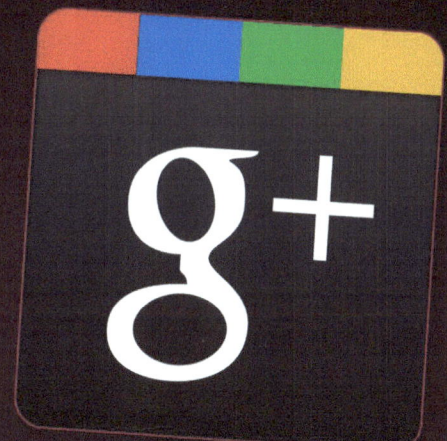

G+ Logo courtesy of Google

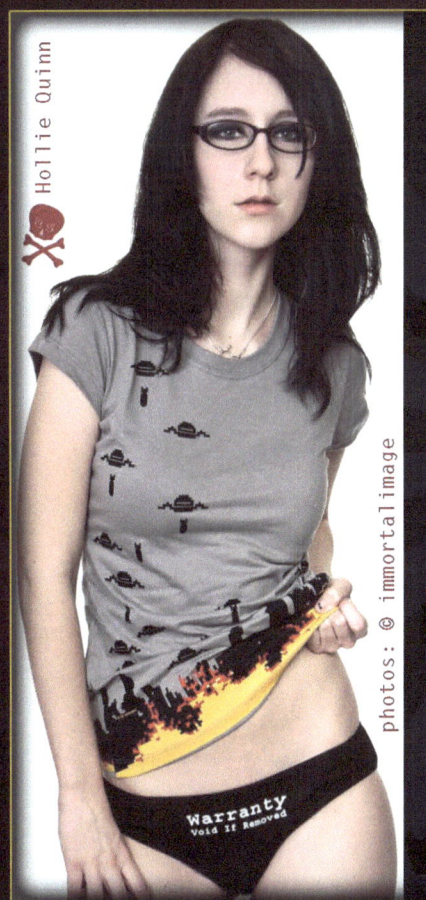
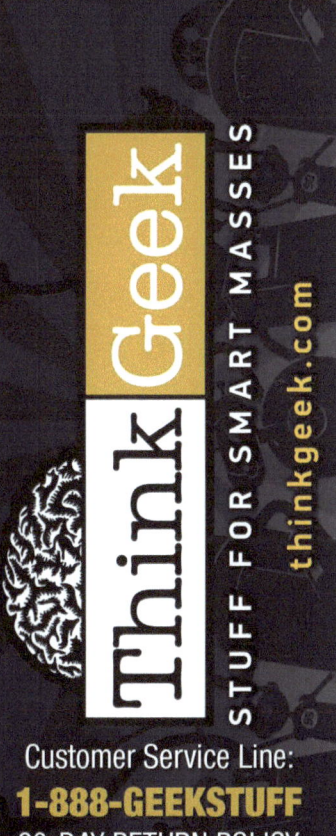
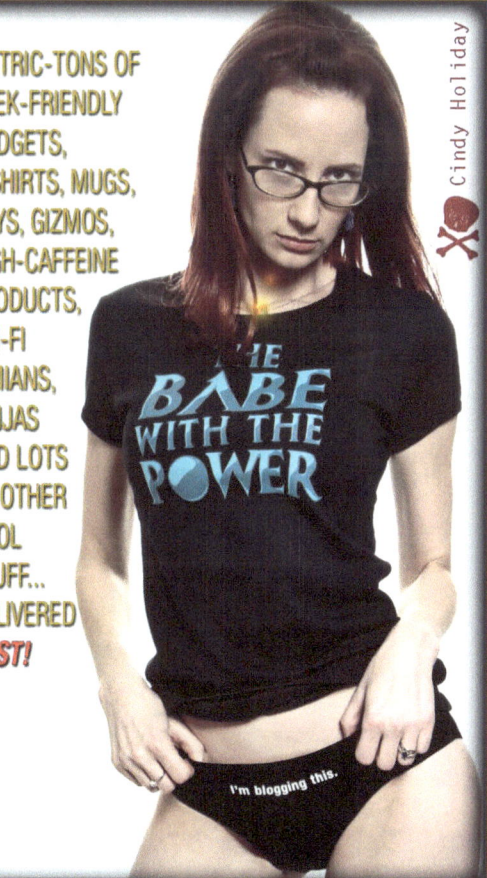

GRAVEYARDGIRL: # LEIGH FOX

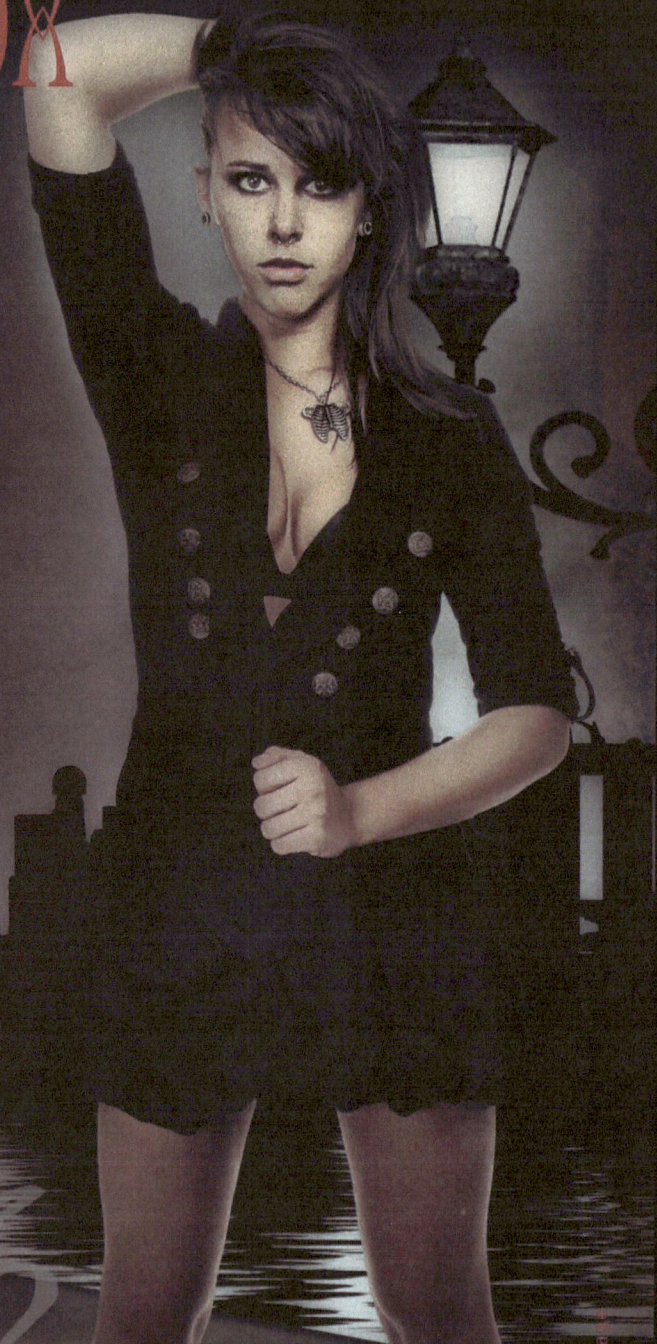

Leigh Fox, "Like the animal, only better" was born in Japan, but is now here in the United States. She tells us she "spent about 10 years out of country," and "some time in Southern California," but "attended high school in Toutle, Washington." She also adds "I miss it. We would spend hours playing at the Columbia River in Kalama where Twilight was filmed, but it was cooler back before that happened."

Her musical tastes include *"anything that fits"* her mood. Some she mentioned were: "old school" Metallica, A Day To Remember, Hollywood Undead, Journey, Chris Brown (*ONLY SOME! Don't JUDGE!*). "Rihanna's new stuff is really awesome."

When it comes to movies, she tells us *"I like kid movies, only because I'm not a kid anymore."* She also adds *"I love intense movies that make you say 'What the hell just happened?!' V for Vendetta is a favorite."*

She also has a special message for our readers. Leigh says *"don't let anybody tell you that you can't be who you are. 'Nobody can make you feel inferior without your consent' - Eleanor Roosevelt. Just reach for the stars and everything else will fall into place."*

Welcome aboard Leigh!

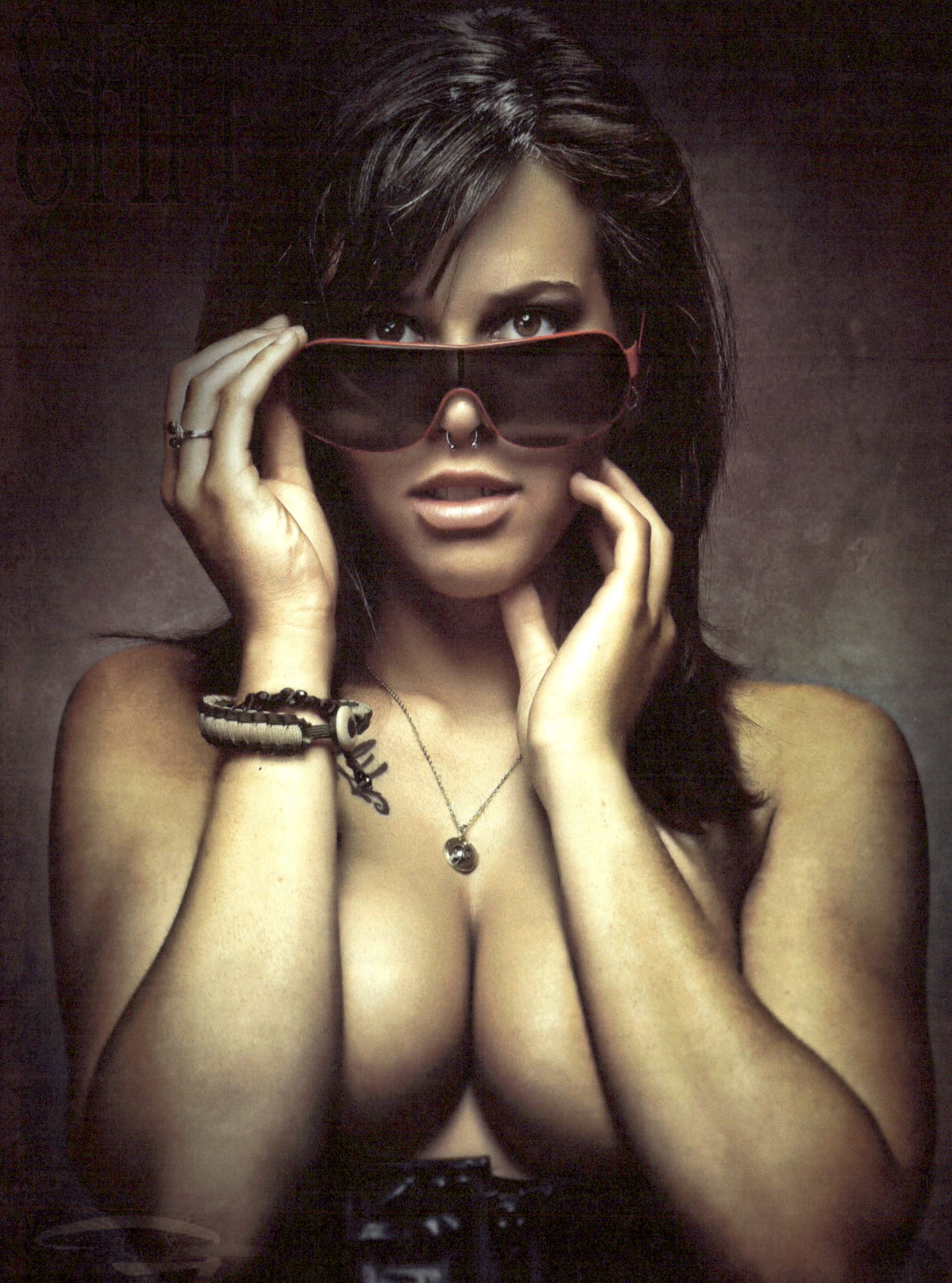

photo: © Justin Kates

GRAVEYARDGIRL: LEIGH FOX

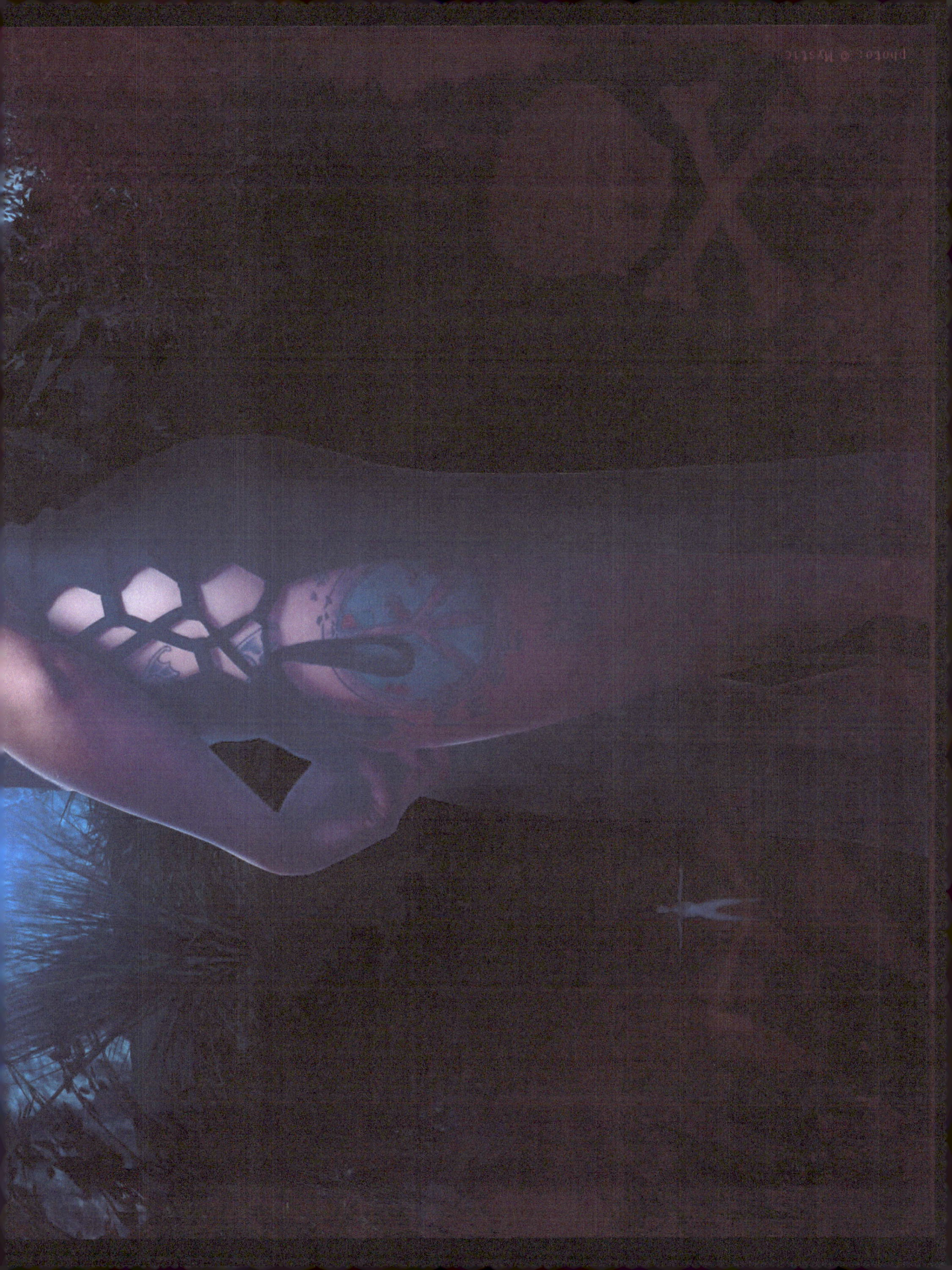

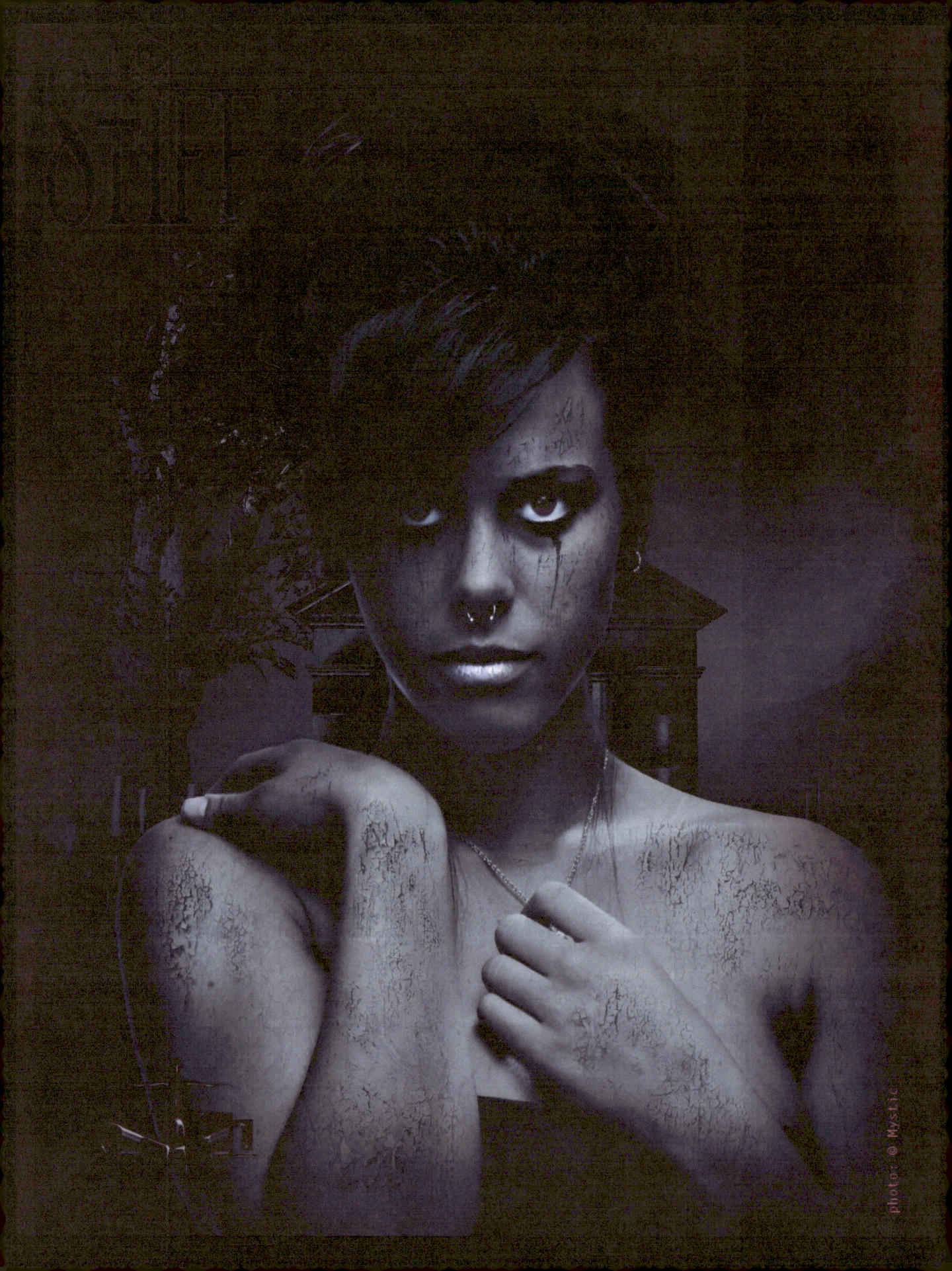

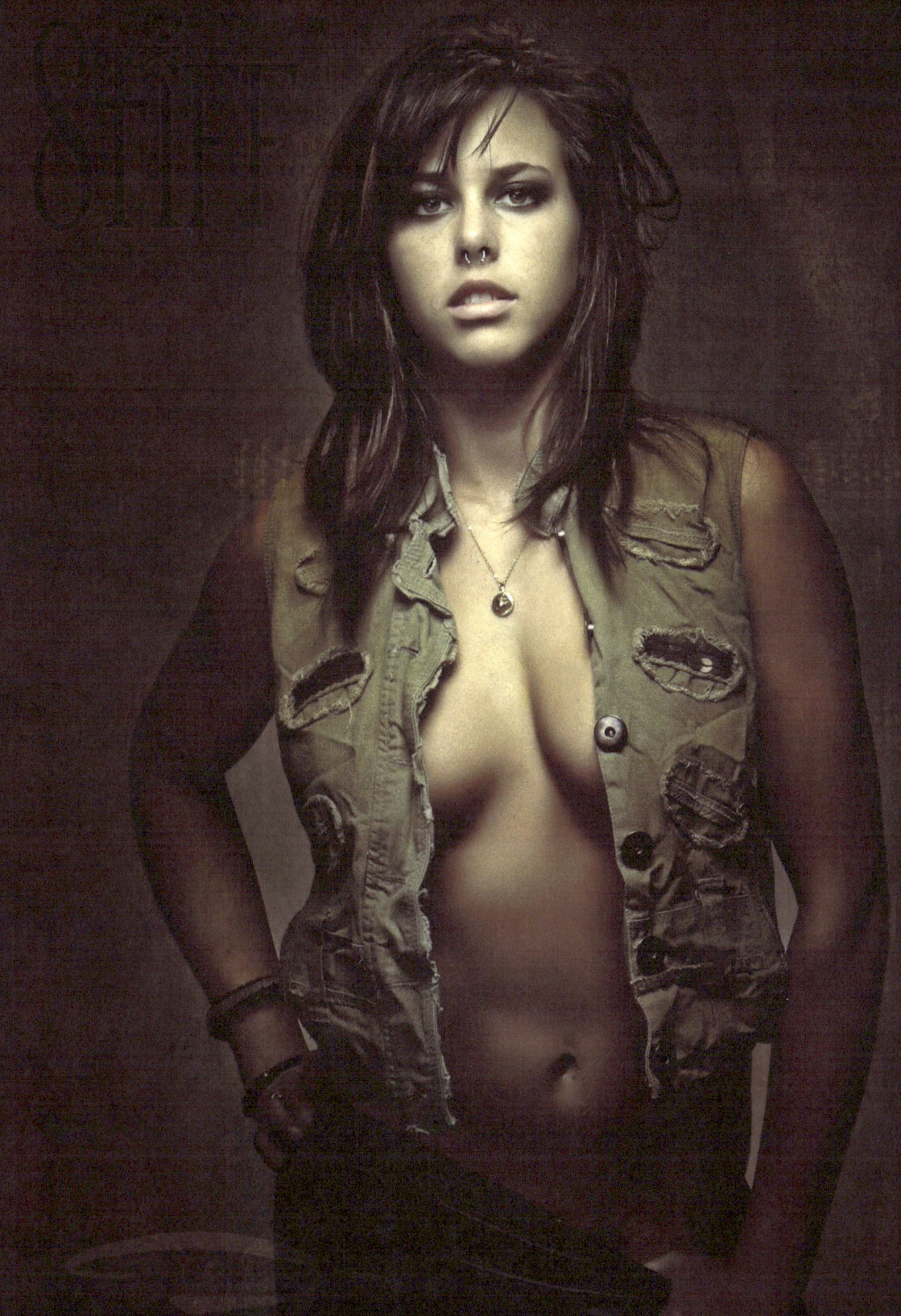

STUDIOS

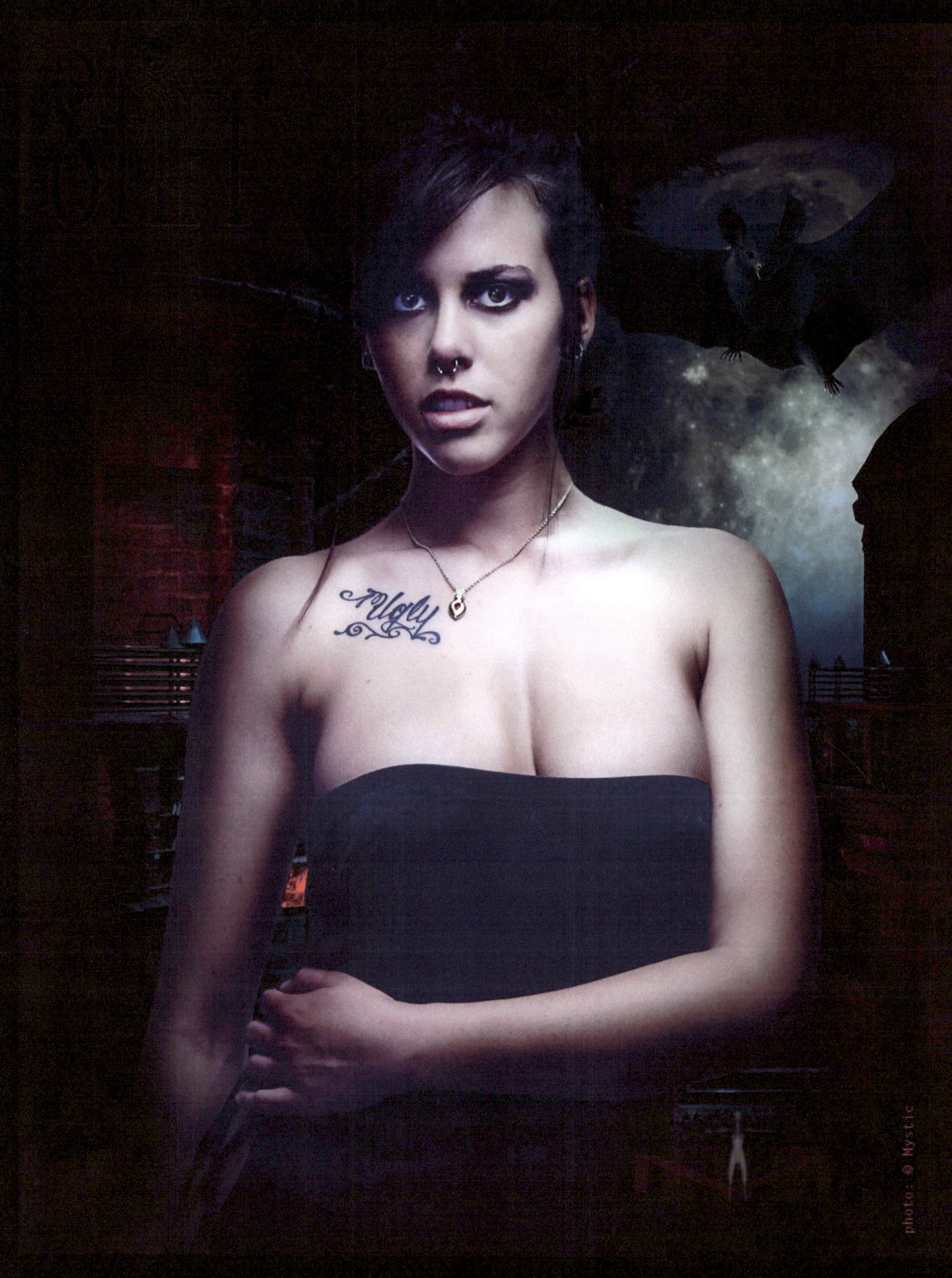

photo: © Mystic

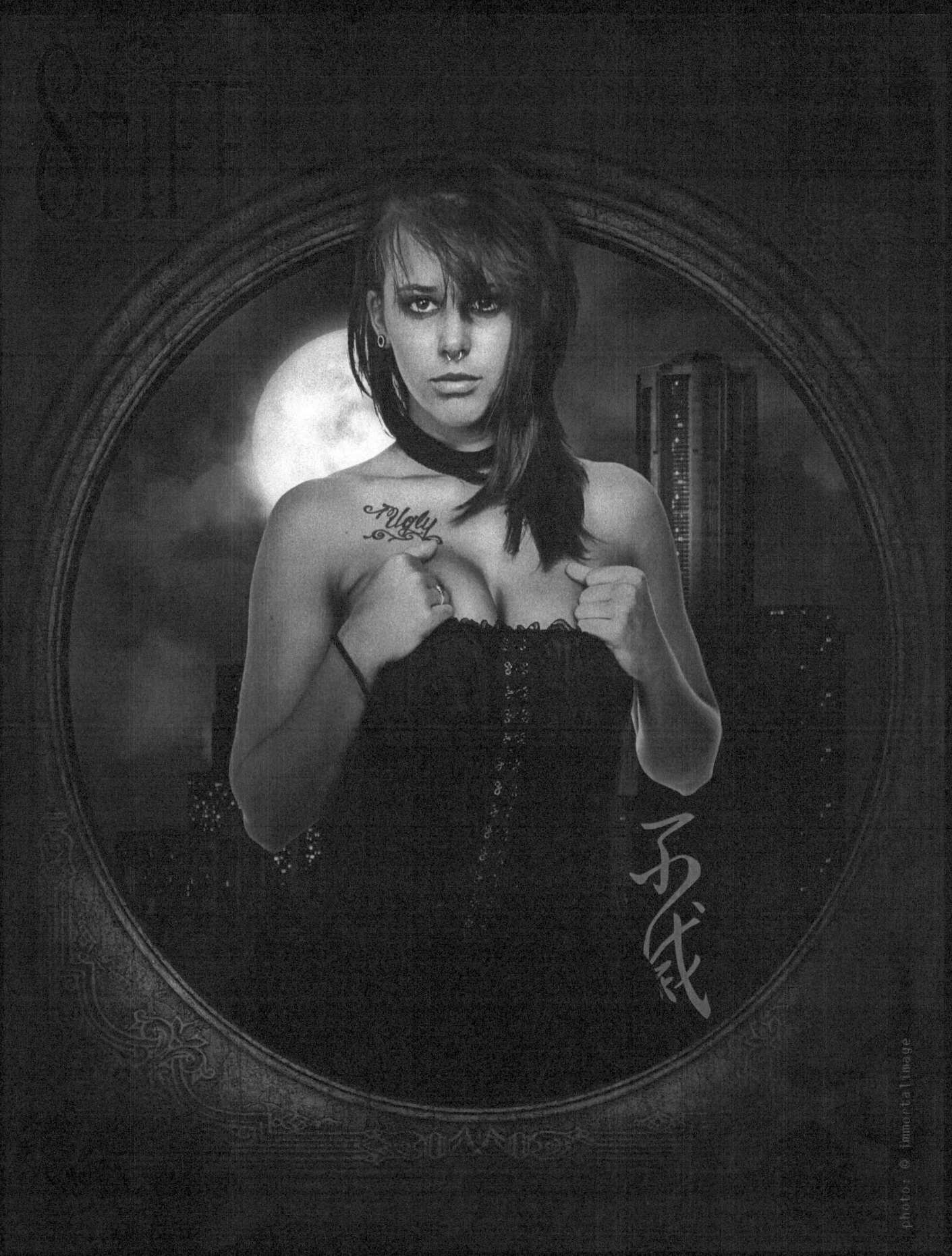

## FEATURE FILM: "FRIGHT NIGHT (2011)"
by: Epic Nguyen

Let's be honest, the original "Fright Night" was far from being a cinematic masterpiece, but it did pull off the difficult trifecta of being funny, freaky and all-around fun. The movie (and so many others like it) has carved out its place in the hallowed hall of fan nostalgia, which is why the notion of remaking the film has been met with ire, anxiety, and more than a bit of annoyance. So, do director Craig Gillespie and his A-list cast manage to make their remake a worthwhile venture, while still honoring that which made the original a cult-classic? The short answer: Pretty much.

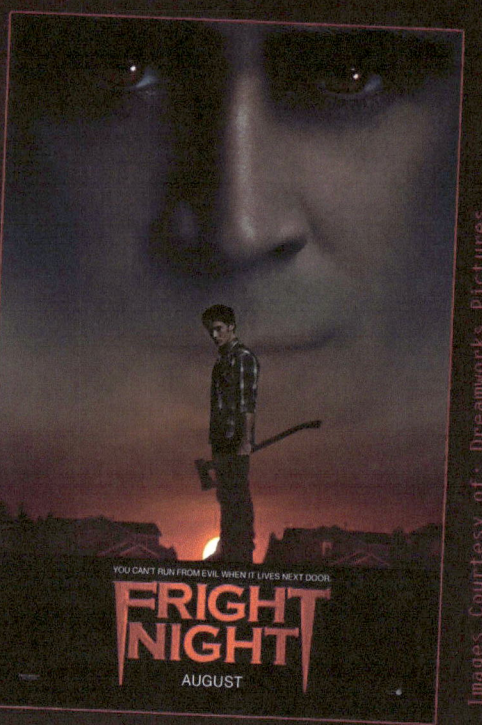

The premise is the same, though the setting has changed: Charley Brewster (Anton Yelchin) lives in a small development community just off the Las Vegas strip. It's a community where people come and go with the desert wind, and many residents are used to a lifestyle of sleeping through the day and working their nights away on the strip - so it's of little portent when more and more of the cookie-cut houses in the development start turning up vacant, or kids from Charley's school get marked down as perpetually absent.

Only one person seems to notice anything strange: Charley's former best friend Ed (Superbad's Christopher Mintz-Plasse), a geeky spaz who Charley has left behind in his climb up the high school social ladder, along with his new girlfriend, Amy. Ed tries to sell Charley on a crazy revelation: that Charley's new neighbor, Jerry (Golden Globe Winner: Colin Farrell), is actually a ferocious vampire who has been preying on their isolated community. Charley, of course, thinks immature Ed is simply "reading too much Twilight."

However, it soon becomes apparent to Charley that Ed may not be so crazy after all. But as Charley realizes the truth about Jerry, Jerry realizes that Charley has learned his secret. From there it becomes a battle for survival, one which Charley cannot win alone… and so he desperately seeks out the most unlikely vampire hunter one could imagine, illusionist Peter Vincent (Doctor Who's David Tennant), to help put Jerry in the grave for good.

If you can't tell from the premise, this is the type of film that relies heavily on tone to avoid collapsing under the weight of its own silliness. Thankfully, director Craig Gillespie knows exactly what this film needs to be: light in the funny parts, tense and gripping in the scary parts, with an undercurrent of playful B-movie tongue-in-cheek throughout the proceedings. It also helps that Gillespie is a very competent director, able to create great set pieces, good action sequences, with a sharp eye for color, lighting, and space. The script is witty, winking and well paced, and Gillespie manages to craft some truly tense and scary moments where appropriate. The general air of self-deprecation keeps the movie fun no matter what is going on, and the cast embraces that sense of kitschy fun in their respective roles.

Anton Yelchin and Colin Farrell are an unlikely, and yet extremely effective, pairing. Yelchin is good about conveying Charley's journey from being an ex-nerd playing cool, to a bug-eyed weirdo stricken with paranoia, to a ballsy fighter determined to protect those he loves. The young actor has skill and range and puts both on display without ever weighing the role down by taking things too seriously. Farell looks like he's having a blast as Jerry, a character that allows him to play up both his pretty boy suaveness and bad boy menace with equal aplomb. It's clear that we're living in an age where the image of the vampire has taken a sharp turn sideways, because seeing a vamp that's nothing but cunning and ruthless is so familiar, and yet, so refreshing. As Ed says at one point, "He's not lovesick, or misunderstood, he's the f**ing shark from 'Jaws'!" And it's a welcome return to form for bloodsuckers everywhere. Farrell chews the scenery (and his victims) and spits out tons of bloody good fun.

One role many fans of the original will be critical of is that of Peter Vincent. The iconic character (originally played by the legendary Roddy McDowall), was as hammy as he was fun. David Tennant steps into the role of Vincent and manages to make it his own, while still keeping the character equally hammy and enjoyable as the original.

Finally, the 3D format of "Fright Night" is well constructed - which is especially impressive, given that a lot of the film takes place at night. 3D tends to dampen color schemes, but not once did the movie get too dark or murky to make out what was going on - nor did it suffer from the depth distortion which plagues other 3D films. On the other hand: a lot of what takes place in the first two-thirds of the film (such as people walking, talking and hanging around everyday environments) doesn't require the added 3D. It isn't until later, when the action kicks into high gear, that there are some truly worthwhile 3D moments. The rest of the time, CGI gore spraying out at the audience is pretty much the extent of the effect's usefulness. I will say this, though: whether purposeful or not, the hokey 3D gore effects do add to the campiness and are just another layer of B-movie fun.

All things considered, "Fright Night" manages to give an old idea a fresh modern spin, but doesn't sacrifice the original's kitschy fun factor as a result. Definitely one of the better horror movie remakes out there, and definitely worth checking out. 4 out of 5 scars.

INDIE FILM: "The Feed"
by: Dave Harlequin

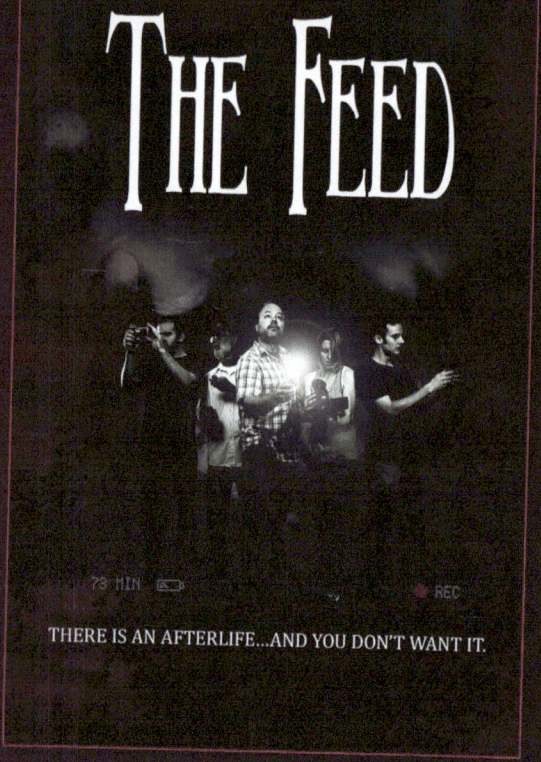

THE FEED

73 MIN      ● REC

THERE IS AN AFTERLIFE...AND YOU DON'T WANT IT.

In the era of reality-television, it seems the "found-footage" sub-genre of horror film, and those paranormal-investigative shows are all the rage. With hit films such as "The Blair Witch Project," "REC," and "Paranormal Activity," and their TV-counterparts such as "Ghost Hunters" and "Paranormal State," it seems everyone really wants to see something spooky. But what if, just once, something horrible actually happened on one of these so-called "reality" shows? Fist in Post Films' latest supernatural thriller "The Feed" finally answers that question.

The popular reality-TV show, "Ghost Chasers" (in celebration of their 4th year on the air) are presenting their annual special-edition live broadcast from the historic Brenway Theatre to investigate numerous reports of paranormal activity. Located in the small-town of Lewisburg, Pennsylvania, the famous movie theatre has a very violent past, which for three generations, has served to fuel many local legends of it being haunted. After a short documentary about the theatre's history, the "Ghost Chasers" staff set up their equipment and get right to work. Before long, the reality-TV crew quickly discovers that the Brenway Theatre is not your average "haunted" location… because this place actually IS haunted by evil spirits!

Writer/Director Steve Gibson does an incredible job of recreating a live ghost-hunting show, right down to the show graphics (mirroring that of SyFy's "Ghost Hunters") and shooting nearly the entire second half of the film in the green monochrome "NightVision" that paranormal reality shows are known for. To top it all off; Gibson even takes the "live TV" feel to a whole new level by adding in fake commercials, one of which features a hilarious cameo by Troma President Lloyd Kaufman as one of those TV injury lawyers. In addition, Gibson, along with his superb cast, does an excellent job of building tension and suspense… right down to film's horrifying (or as us horror fans call it, satisfying) ending!

Shot on a budget of only $10,000, "The Feed" does an amazing job of making the most out of it's limited budget, not least of which hiring an excellent cast of newcomers, who really bring the film to life with their very believable reactions and very natural execution of the well-written script. The "Ghost Chasers" host Brian Pollack (played by Chip Facka) acts as a narrator through most of the film, adding to the suspension of disbelief, and keeping the viewer right there with them as the terror unfolds. Combine that with top-notch cinematography and post-production, and you've got one of the best independent films I've seen in a very long time.

Recently, "The Feed" has seen quite a bit of success, including winning the coveted award for "Best Feature" at the 2011 Famous Monsters of Filmland: "Imagi-Movies Film Festival" in Beverly Hills, California. The film is currently available on a limited DVD run via Fist in Post Films, and should see a mass-release very soon. Check out their official website at: www.thefeedmovie.com for more info and updates on DVD availability.

Overall, "The Feed" really sets the standard and raises the bar for indie filmmaking. It's a very well done and highly entertaining supernatural thriller that will leave you on the edge of your seat from start to finish. Highly recommended, especially for fans of the subgenre.
On the indie-scale: we give it a full 5 out of 5 scars!

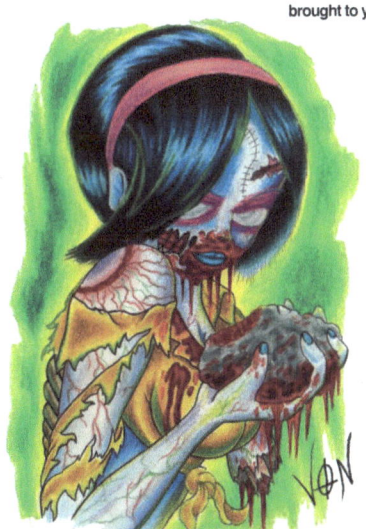

RETRO FILM: "The Lost Boys"
by: Dave Harlequin

1987's teen vampire flick "The Lost Boys" isn't exactly the scariest horror movie ever made. In fact, the ridiculously over-sized 80s hairstyles are probably more frightening than the fangs. Come to think of it, it's not exactly the funniest comedy you're ever likely to come across either. But there's just something about its 50-50 mix of the two genres that just works fantastically well, creating a memorable nocturnal cult-classic that manages to amount to much more than the sum of its parts.

The main focus of the film is the Emerson family. Mom (Diane Wiest) has just split up with her husband, so along with her two sons Michael and Sam (Jason Patric and the late Corey Haim), she drives to the seaside town of Santa Carla to stay with Grandpa (Barnard Hughes, who you 80s kids might also remember as the Gramps out of 'Blossom'). One night, the family is all out, enjoying a nice evening of live rock power ballads (what a soundtrack this one's got, by the way), when Michael spots himself a longhaired lovely by the name of Star (Jami Gertz). He follows her for a while, gets introduced to her motorcycle-riding vampire friends (among them a mullet-crowned Kiefer Sutherland, in his breakthrough role) and, long story short, he becomes a vampire. And that, kids, is why you're not supposed to wander off with strangers!

Despite its fairly conservative running time of just over an hour-and-a-half, there are loads going on in this film. Alongside Michael's delve into the world of transition-vamp (not to be confused with a full-vamp), there's a blossoming romance between Mom and creepy video store owner Max (Edward Herrmann), a couple of brothers (Corey Feldman and Jamison Newlander) who claim to be the local experts on bloodsucker-busting, and even a bit of space at the side for that one guy who played in the 'Bill & Ted' movies (Alex Winter, who never really did as well as Keanu Reeves, did he?).

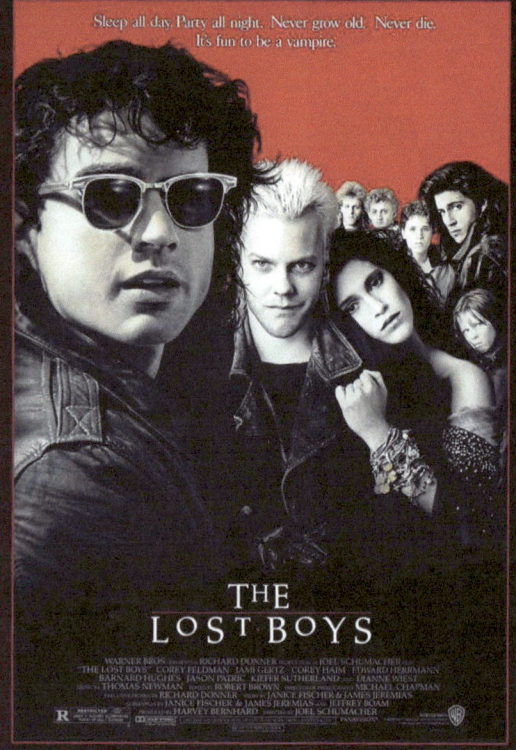

Sleep all day. Party all night. Never grow old. Never die.
It's fun to be a vampire.

THE LOST BOYS

WARNER BROS. presents a RICHARD DONNER production a JOEL SCHUMACHER film
THE LOST BOYS · COREY FELDMAN · JAMI GERTZ · COREY HAIM · EDWARD HERRMANN
BARNARD HUGHES · JASON PATRIC · KIEFER SUTHERLAND and DIANNE WIEST
music THOMAS NEWMAN executive ROBERT BROWN director MICHAEL CHAPMAN
produced RICHARD DONNER story JAN FISCHER & JAMES JEREMIAS
screenplay JANICE FISCHER & JAMES JEREMIAS and JEFFREY BOAM
produced HARVEY BERNHARD directed JOEL SCHUMACHER

Images Courtesy of: Warner Home Video

It's pure popcorn stuff, of course. It's not saying anything profound, and it's certainly not trying to teach us anything… but let's be honest, if you're after that sort of thing you're hardly likely to settle down with a Joel Schumacher movie anyway. What it is, though, is an extremely entertaining goth-romp featuring some very black comedy, tongue-in-cheek performances all around, and just enough climactic gore to go out with a bang.
Warner Home Video released "The Lost Boys" in the most current form of a 2-disc Special Edition DVD. It features a director's commentary; deleted scenes, a retrospective documentary, a multi-angle featurette on "The Lost Coreys" (Haim and Feldman), four "Inside the Vampire's Cave" features, and a behind-the-scenes feature on the work of make-up master Greg Cannom. For all you HD types, it's also available on Blu-Ray with all the same special features.

Overall, "The Lost Boys" is one of the true gems of the 1980s. It never once takes itself too seriously, but it doesn't make fun of itself either, making for an entertaining film, that's just good old-fashioned fun. It's a true cult-classic that (even knocking on the door of its 25th anniversary) never seems to get old, and did we mention the fact that it has a killer soundtrack? If you have somehow never seen this film, put down this magazine and go watch it right now. And please folks, if you have kids, make them watch this instead of the "Twilight" saga. We'd all really appreciate it.

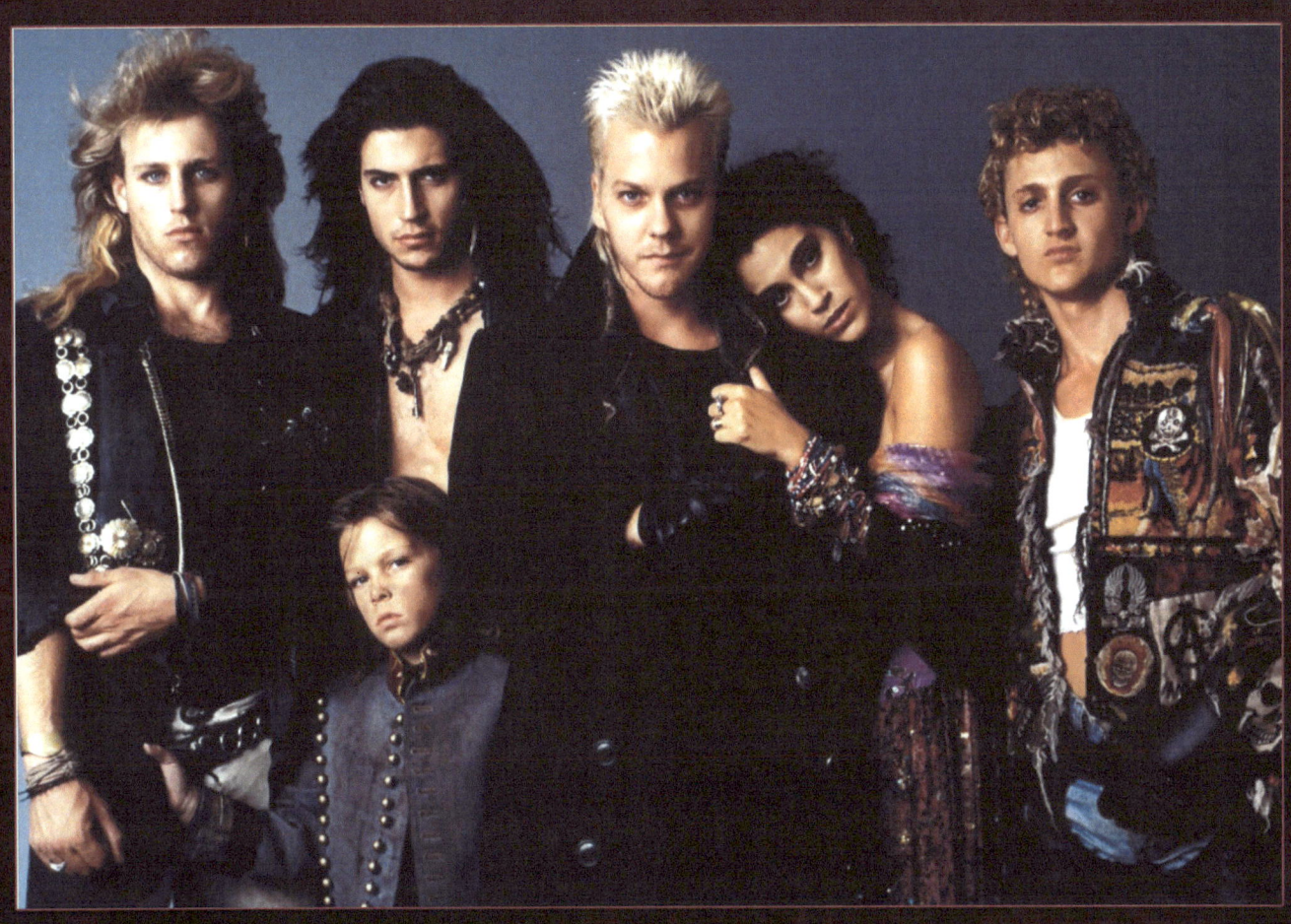

ARI LEHMAN:
"Three Decades of Terror: a few words with the original
Jason Voorhees"
by: Dave Harlequin

*Thank you so much for taking the time to sit down with us. First off, you were only 14 years old when you first took on the iconic role of Jason Voorhees. How did you get the part?*
"Greetings From CAMP CRYSTAL LAKE, Dave, to you, the gorgeous GRAVEYARD GIRLS, and all the Horror Vixens and Warriors who read STIFF MAGAZINE! I consider it a great honor to do an interview for this electrifying and progressive publication. Also, as F13 fans now know so well, I consider it a great honor to have portrayed the first young Jason Voorhees in the now-classic horror feature, Friday The 13th when I was 14 years old. I in fact got the role through a mixture of sheer luck and naïve audacity.

When I was very young, my Father took me to see "Star Wars" in Times Square, NYC. I was thrilled. After that I wanted to be in a movie more than anything. I was studying music, and I would play the theme from "Star Wars" on the piano every day, over and over again. I went back to see it nine times when it arrived in the town we lived in, Westport, Connecticut.

The lucky part is, the great movie director, Sean S. Cunningham, also happened to live in Westport, and had his offices there as well. I heard about an audition at the Westport YMCA, and I made up my mind to just walk right in there and audition. I came up with the idea of bringing a clip-board with me to look official. No one batted an eye when I approached the front desk, and asked, 'where is the audition?' 'Go on upstairs', was the answer, and I did without hesitation. I was handed a fat script, read several times for Sean, and landed an 80-line role in "Manny's Orphans", a family comedy about inner-city kids who play soccer. We shot this film in Westport and Bridgeport, CT. Perhaps due to the lack of interest in Soccer at the time (1979), that film did not do very well. Sean needed to come up with a new concept quickly to stay on top of the Hollywood game. He was inspired by the success of (John Carpenter's) 'Halloween', and came up with a title alone: Friday The 13th.

After author Victor Miller, set the story in a Summer Camp, they created a scenario involving the drowning of a neglected special-needs camper, who was the son of the camp cook, Pamela Voorhees. So they needed a kid who was the right size. The idea of using Noel Cunningham, Sean's son, was turned down by Sean's wife. Then, Producer Steve Miner suggested me, remembering that I was an open-minded and enthusiastic young actor. Sean called me up at home, and said, 'come over to the office, we have another role for you' Of course I was happy to hear it. 'We do have one important question to ask you first though - can you swim?' 'Yes!' I replied. 'OK you got the part!' laughed Sean S. Cunningham, and the rest is Horror History! I guess being a good swimmer has its advantages!"

What are some of your favorite memories from working on the film?

"By far the best part for me was working together with FX master Tom Savini and his assistant Taso Stavrakos to make the original Jason Voorhees latex mask. Being on the set was a thrill, and I learned a lot there, but visiting Savini's studio was like entering Merlyn's Workshop. One important thing about F13 and Jason Voorhees that many people do not know is that the famous final scene, which gave birth to the monster Jason Voorhees, was not in the original script at all. The ending was to have been on the beach, after the fight to the death between Alice Hardy and Pamela Voorhees, not in the lake. Then Sean saw 'Carrie', and decided that he wanted a similar surprise ending for F13. He asked Victor Miller and the rest of the crew to come up with ideas, and so the story goes, Savini, wanting to go further with the Boy in the Lake idea, came up with the famous final scene concept, ultimately a riff off of 'Creature from the Black Lagoon', 'Jaws' and 'Dementia 13'. I was called to do the scene in October, which was where the fun really started, because I actually got to jump up out of the water and drag Alice Hardy back in, (taking) revenge for decapitating Mother! I definitely had fun pretending to drown in the first scene, and now it was as if someone handed me a fantasy-come-true, both as an actor and for the character Jason himself, now victorious!

The script they handed me, however, read 'Alice's Dream'. 'What?' I asked Tom Savini, 'this is NOT a dream! It is real!' I insisted. Tom said, 'Well, how do you expect Jason to have survived for 11 years under the water?' 'Easy!' I said, being a total Sci-Fi/Fantasy/Comic fan at the time, 'Jason survives like Swamp Thing, like Aquaman, like Creature from the Black Lagoon...like Gollum from Lord of the Rings!' I declared. 'Ari, Tom Savini in 1979, being truly creative and generously open-minded, 'if you SEE it as real, PLAY it as real, because a ghost in a dream believes it's real too.' I accepted that, because to me, even now, a ghost in a dream is very real. Some would say that in the long run my view has held true, since Jason Voorhees is most certainly not a dream at all, unlike his famous foe!"

What's it like being part of a character and movie that has become so beloved amongst horror fans?

"I am humbled every day to be identified with the vast and powerful Mythos of Jason Voorhees. The fans of Jason and F13 are the most devoted fans in the world, and I have found this to be true far and wide, in both urban and rural locations. Because of these fans, Jason Voorhees has somehow

## ARI LEHMAN (Continued)

become a new American archetype of our unconscious, as all enduring myths and legends truly are, because they reveal (both) the champions of our greatest hopes and the demons of our greatest fears. It's an absolutely surreal experience for me; maybe that's why I have so much fun with it. I am deeply grateful to the fans that through FIRSTJASON we have musically manifested a tangible means by which others may share in this thrill ride, this inside joke, and I am to be forever in their debt for helping me to alchemically transform my figurehead role into an ever-evolving platform of sound. The fans created FIRSTJASON as much as I did."

*You do a lot of horror conventions and live appearances, what are some of your favorite ones to go to?*

"I urge everyone to support all of the Horror Conventions in their area. I have been welcomed by almost all of the events at one time or another, and I encourage all of their efforts. I also want everyone to go support the Haunted Attractions, Horror-Punk/Rock and Metal Fests, as well as Goth Art and Tattoo Conventions. There is really an explosion of Dark Arts across the board: HorrorHound Weekend, Spooky Empire, Monster Mania, ScareFest, Crypticon, and of course Comic Con and DragonCon are BIG! (And) two new events that deserve notice are Motor City Nightmares Weekend in Detroit and Days of the Dead in Indianapolis, both of whom have invited FIRSTJASON to rock the house this year. We traveled to France in July, to perform at Bloody Weekend in Audincourt, and we have appeared at several events throughout Holland & Germany sponsored by Needful Specials."

*Your band FIRSTJASON has really been making a big impact among the under-ground horror & music scenes… tell us a bit about your band, how did FIRSTJASON get started?*

"FIRSTJASON was born out of a desire to create a sound cut from a darker cloth. Back in the early 80's, while studying Jazz Piano at NYU, I would go to CBGB'S to see Bad Brains, Dead Kennedys, and my good friends, the band Reagan Youth. I enjoyed Motorhead and Danzig concerts back then, and went to see White Zombie, and GWAR several times. I felt that music similar to this would best represent Jason's inner rage. I called upon the help of my old friend from the NYC Punk Scene, (former Cro-Mags drummer) Cleaver; Cleaver (aka Amit Shamir) is a multi-talented drummer, and also a professional vegan chef. Then we were joined by Nefarious (aka Chuck Lescewicz) the bassist for Macabre. Nefarious helped us to streamline the band's sound, and he is the one who suggested that I create a special keytar.

2009 saw the release of (debut album) 'Jason is Watching!' that came out on the same day as the new 'Friday The 13th', February 13th. The album recorded and mastered at Sonic Palace Studios by Matt Mercado. FIRSTJASON was recently signed to Dark Star Records here in Chicago, and we will be releasing another album soon."

*FIRSTJASON has a really cool concept behind it, almost as if it's some-thing of a voice for Jason Voorhees, any thoughts on that description?*

"Jason Voorhees is the Silent Slasher. Songs like 'Machete Is My Friend', 'Jason Never Dies', 'You Better Run' and 'Red Red Red' reveal the workings of the deranged mind of Jason. FIRSTJASON truly IS the voice of Jason. We take the music and concept seriously, but not ourselves. There is a healthy dose of comedy in our approach. Also, there's the instrument that I created after Nefarious urged me to invent the Heavy Metal Keytar: THE KEYCHETE! The Keychete is a Keytar that looks like a Machete, with a LED Jason Mask in the blade, created by FX wizards The Brothers Rich. It sounds like a metal bass guitar and it literally shakes the rafters. The creation of the Keychete, and my utilizing its double-handed approach, while singing simultaneously is both visually and musically appealing, and it displays some athletics that I am certain Jason would be proud of!"

You've played gigs all over the world, what are some of your favorite shows you've played?

"Singing for a Live European TV Broadcast in a magnificent Opera House in Orvieto, Italy, in front of Dario Argento, Robert Englund, Mario Bava, Ruggero Deodato and Jaume Balaguro at the Fantasy Horror Awards Ceremony is definitely one of them. Also, performing outdoors under the stars near Barcelona, Spain for the Festival De Cine De Horror was a great thrill.

Once I was at The Olde Angel in Nottingham, UK and the owner, who plays with The Verucas, asked me to do a memorably wild solo set. Speaking of wild solo sets, once at Weekend of Horrors in Bottrop, Germany, I was gratified when Danny Trejo himself jumped up onstage, did the 'Machete' move with his jacket, and, pointing to the Keychete, said, 'That is F---ing AWESOME!' driving the German crowd absolutely CRAZY! Also, opening for Chimaera at Savage Fest in Green Bay, WI was unforgettable, as was opening for Lordi and Mushroomhead at Rock n Shock in Worcester, MA and Dr. Destruction's Haunted Corn Maze in Kenosha, WI, where we performed live in a cornfield, surrounded by happy families and the October pumpkin harvest! The friends and fans of Lil' Jason are everywhere, so must be FIRSTJASON!"

Musically speaking, who are some of your biggest influences?

"It all started with Jazz for me, so it was Miles Davis, Charles Mingus and John Coltrane for awhile. Then Jimi Hendrix and Bob Marley, and then were the big keyboardists, like Keith Emerson and Rick Wakeman. I always like to listen to the great organist Jimmy Smith too. As for Jazz Piano players, Hank Jones, McCoy Tyner, Hampton Hawes, Sonny Clark, and then there's the ultimate great: Duke Ellington!

When I was learning about Punk, I really listened to Dead Kennedys and Bad Brains incessantly, but The Misfits, Danzig and Motorhead became my faves. Delving deeper into Metal grew a fondness for Deep Purple and Black Sabbath. Also, watching Chicago Death-Metal heroes Macabre perform live has had a profound effect on my approach to live shows. I strongly recommend seeing them to any Metal fan. The synergy and musicianship of this amazing band has to be seen to be believed, and gives a glimpse of the greatness."

In addition to "Friday The 13th" you've done a bit of other film work in recent years… can you tell us a bit about your return to the screen?

"I have indeed enjoyed a return to the Independent Horror Screen, especially as a Soundtrack Composer for 'Vampire: The Movie', a Documentary that received the Rondo Hatton Classic Horror Award for Best Independent Film of 2007. Also, I have portrayed some interesting characters, from

## ARI LEHMAN (Continued)

Delbert Eaton in 'Thanxgiving', to The Circuit Maker in 'Hell-Ephone' to the Backwoods Whorehouse Owner Ray Rae, in 'Terror Overload: Tales From Satan's Trickstop'. These films are great fun, and I always enjoy working together with Indy Producers to create them, and support their efforts."

*Finally, what's next for Ari Lehman? Any new/upcoming film and/or music projects that you're working on?*
"Well all of my travels have led to an idea that have become a Travel Show: 'Dark Travels with Ari Lehman' is a project that is already in the works with hours of footage of fascinatingly mysterious locations that I have visited all over the US and Europe, as well as interviews with top horror actors, writers, directors, and the creators of underground subculture. I invite your readers to join us, and become a 'Dark Travels' Trail Guide by submitting locations at our Facebook Page and website www.DarkTravels.com!

FIRSTJASON is writing material for the new album, most notably the title track 'Jason's Bride' and we will be releasing a special music video to go with it. I have also been cast in three lead roles this year in independent horror productions. 'Tribute' shot in NYC, and 'The Holler' which shoots in Ohio later this year, as well as the 'Jezebeth' TV Series, produced by our record label here in the Chicago area. I must keep the rest a secret, as you know...shhh!

Many Thanks from CAMP CRYSTAL LAKE to Stiff Magazine and your readers, and remember: JASON NEVER DIES!!! "

*For more on Ari Lehman, FIRSTJASON, and all the wild happenings at "Camp Crystal Lake" check out Ari's official website at: www.firstjason.com*

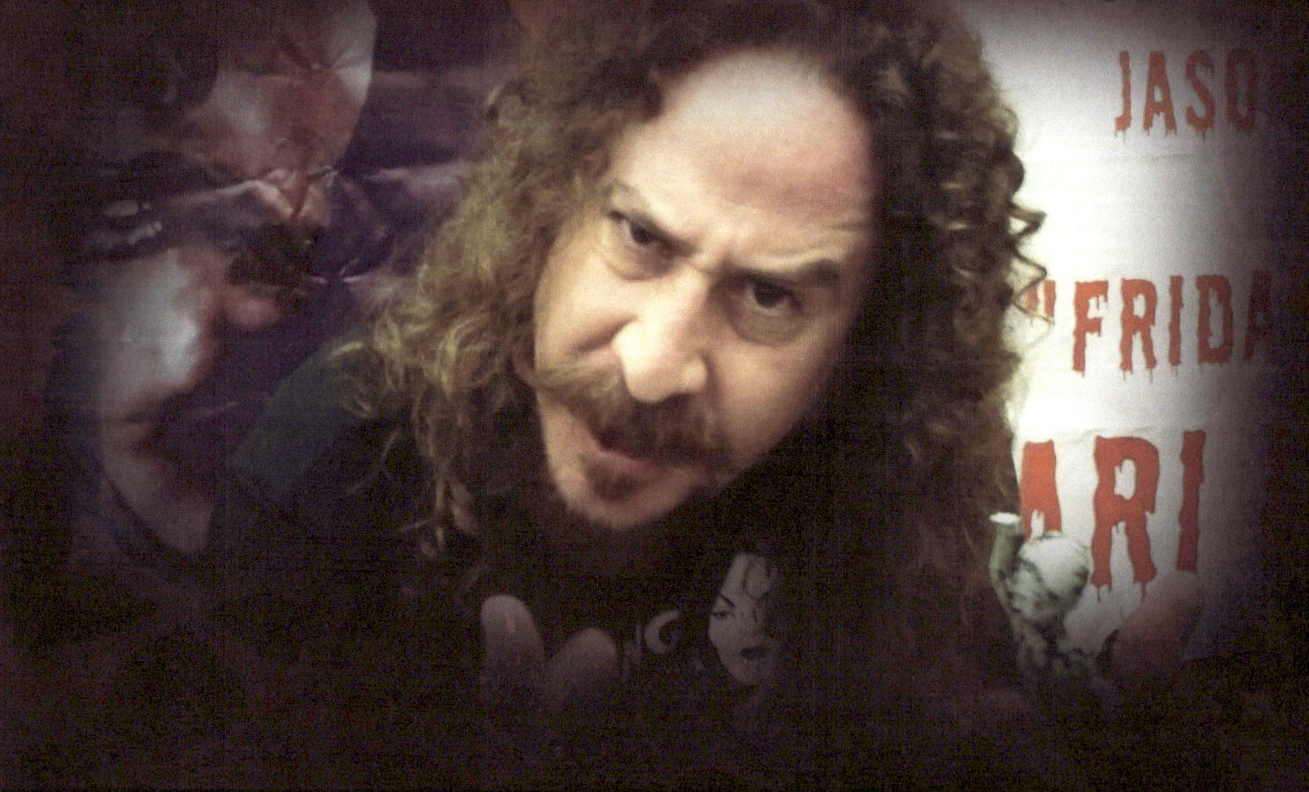

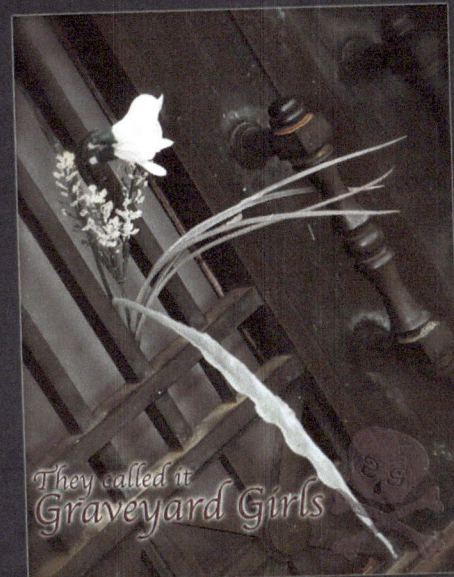
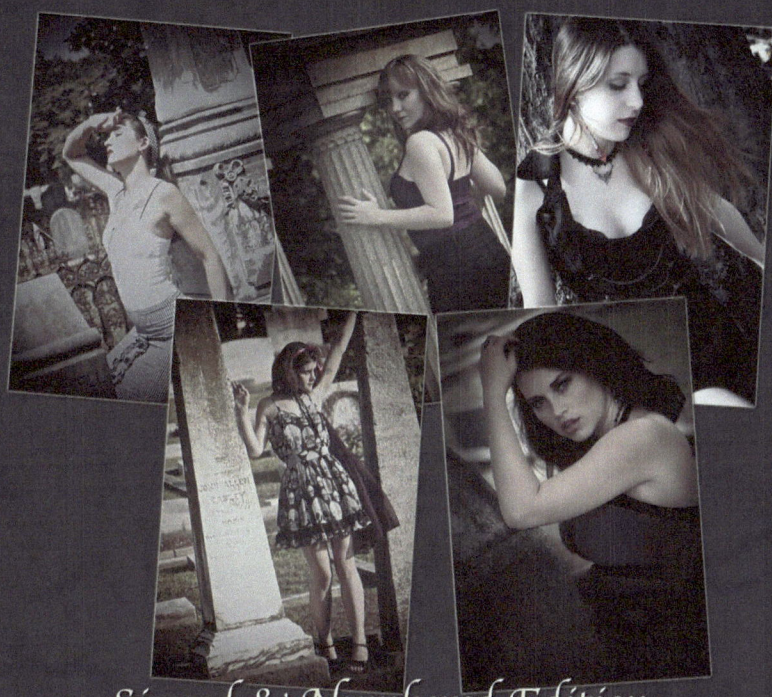

GRAVEYARDGIRL: **COREY**

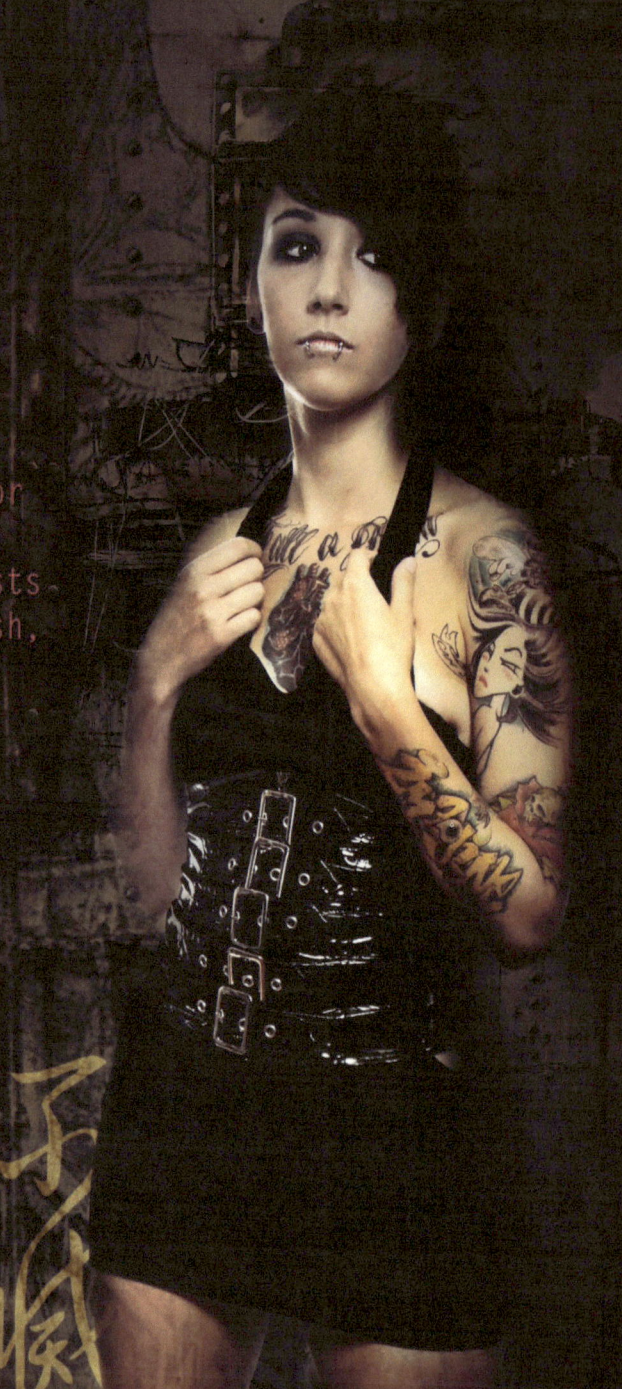

Corey McGovern has been modeling for 5 years and hails from Charlotte, North Carolina. Her primary interests in the field are with pin-up, fetish, and biker fashion modeling.

Musical interests include a wide range. She can listen to "classic rock such as Queen and Aerosmith" one day, but switch to "electronic and country music" the next.

She also tells us "I've been a tattooing and piercing pro for over 3 years. Gogo danced for over 4 years for events such as DJ Keoki, Lady Gaga and Semi Precious Weapons, Shiprocked, Purgatory, Shock Pop, etc."

She also adds "I enjoy long walks on the beach alone... pretending I'm a Sith lord and fishing!"

Oh yes! One of us!

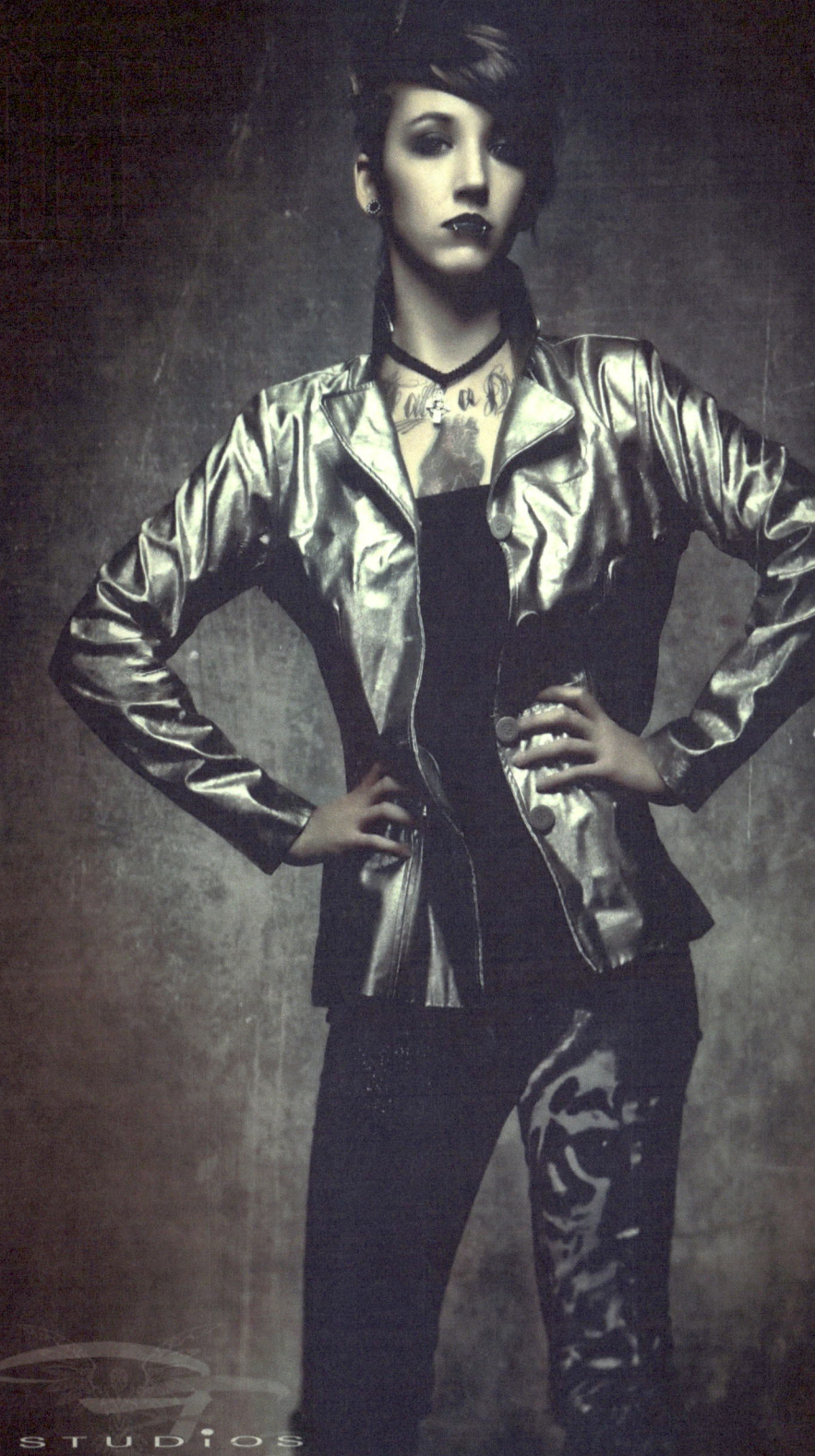

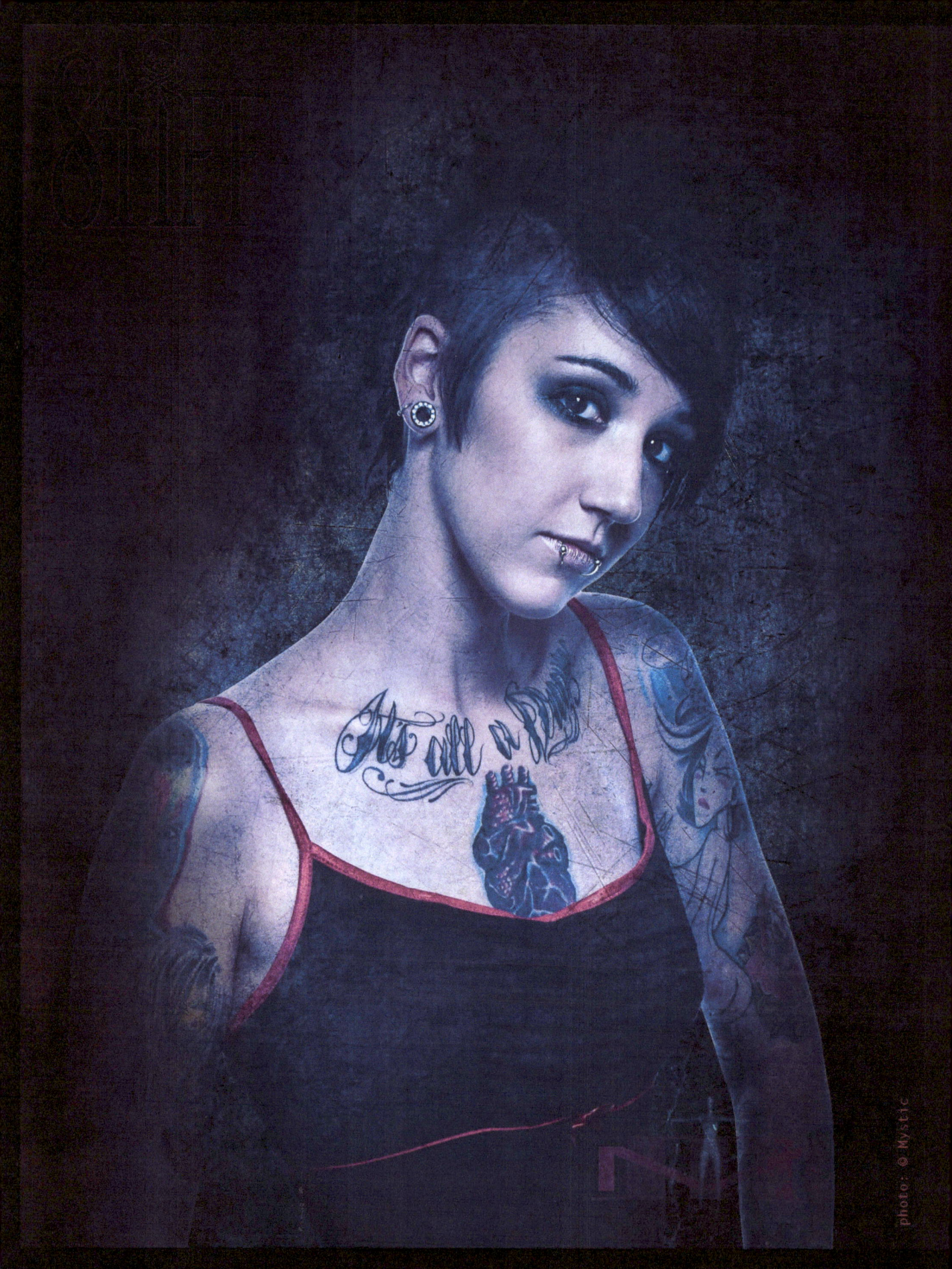

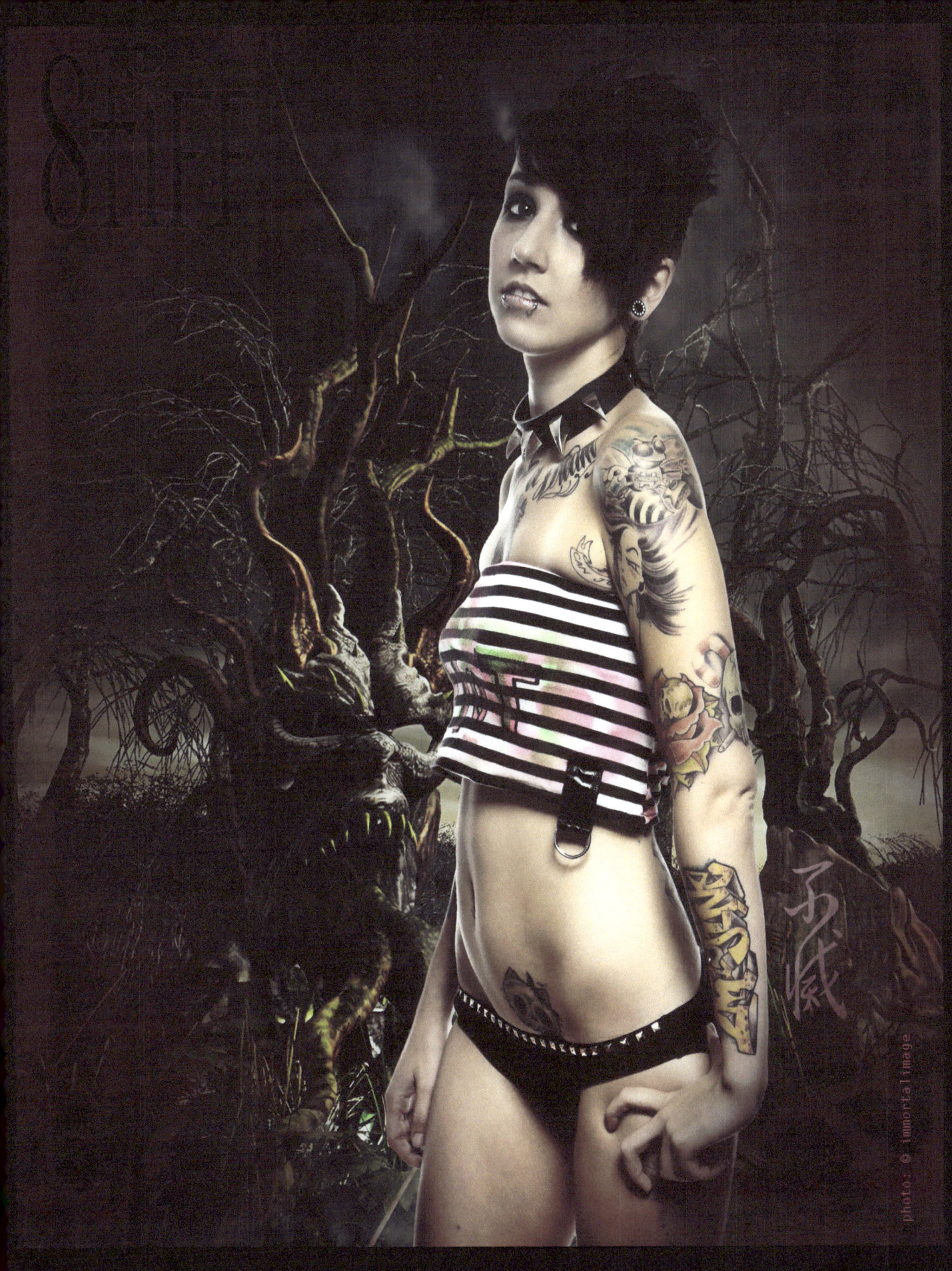

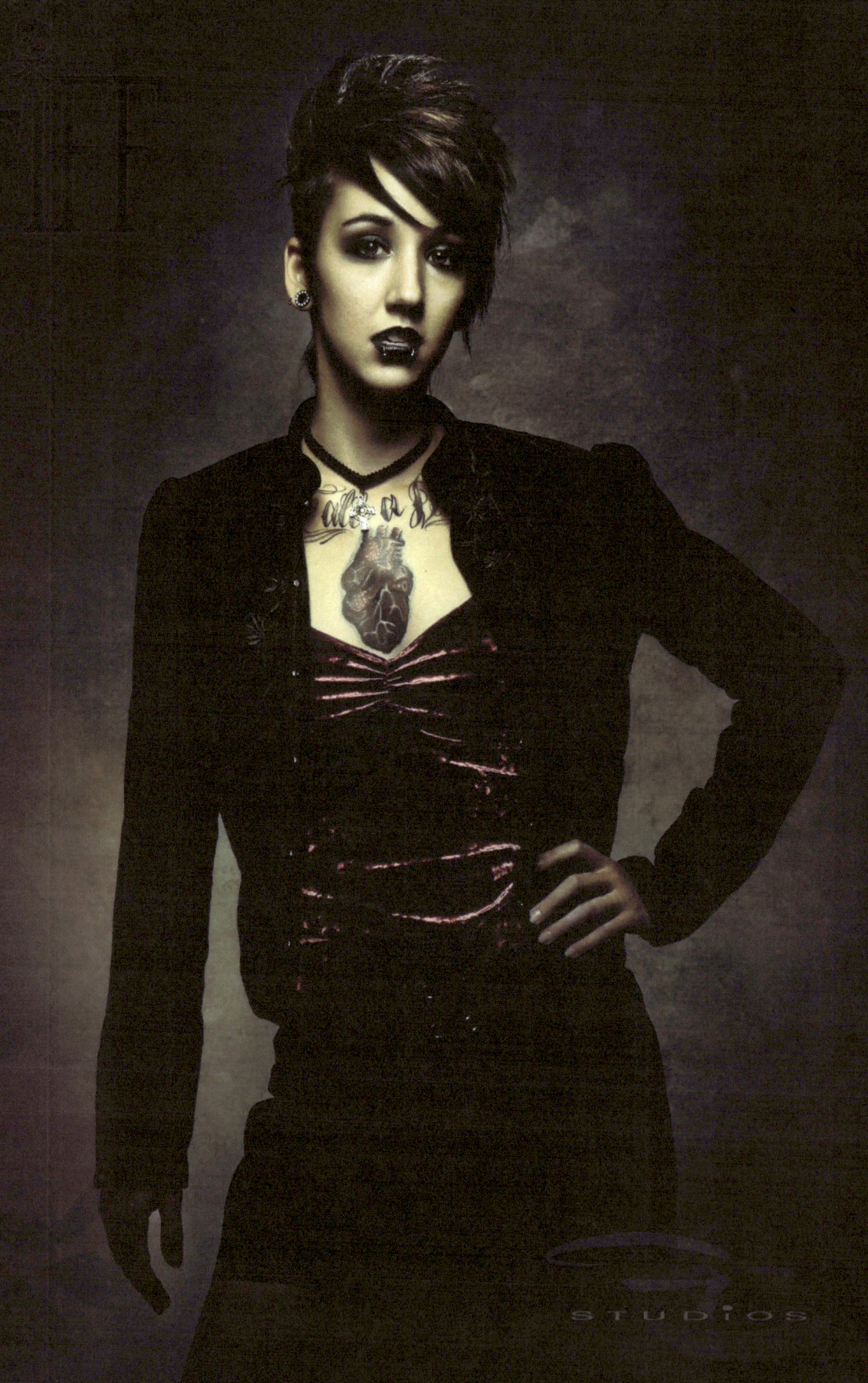

STiFF

STUDiOS

photo: © Justin Kates

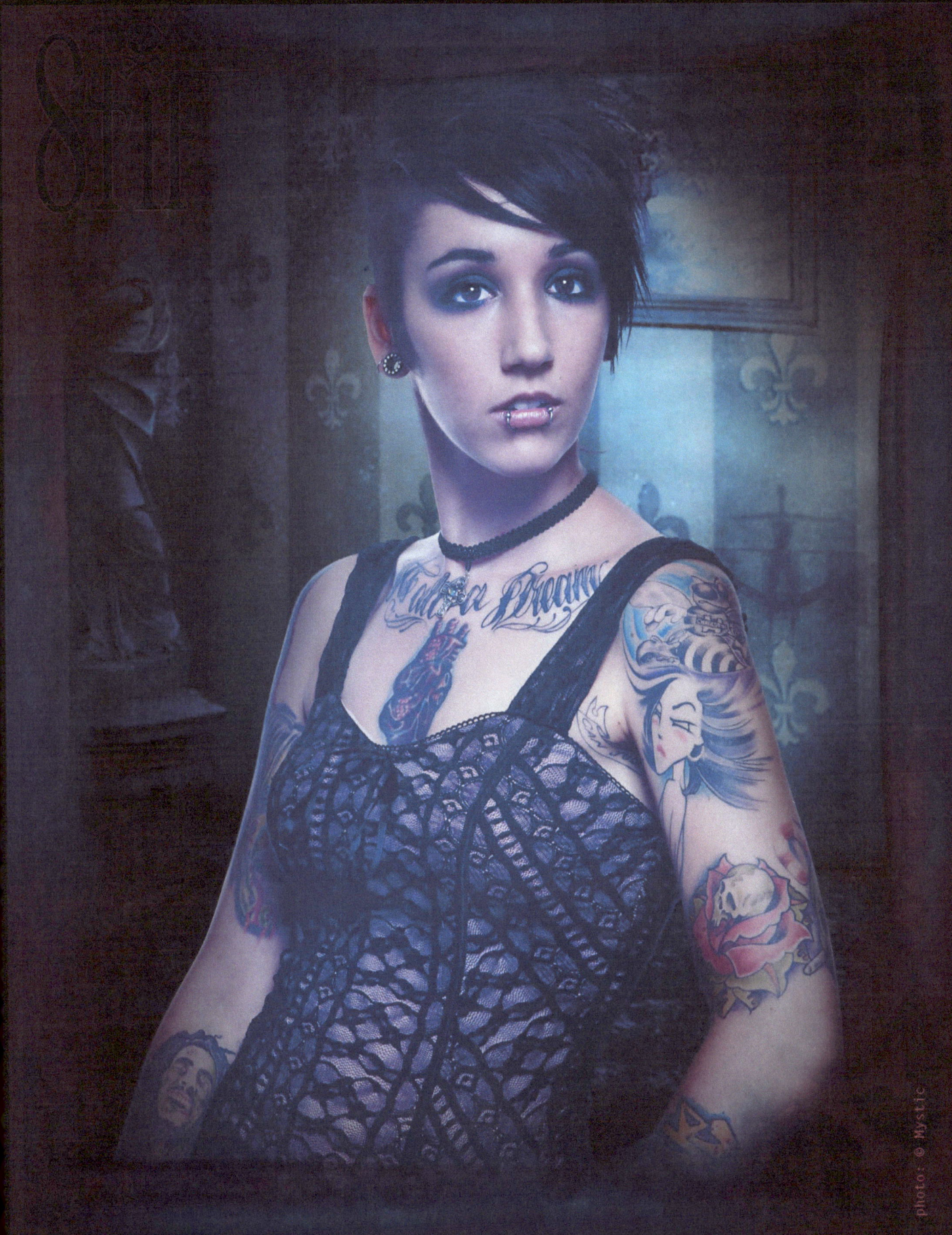

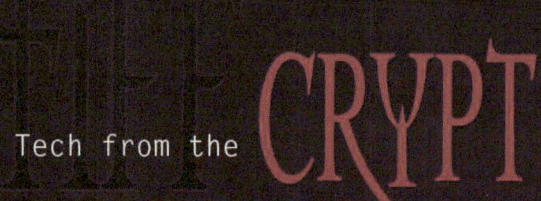

## WTF is an NFC!?!
by: Antigone Kilma

Let's talk about NFCs. No, not some dangerous chemical that'll turn you into a zombie. NFC stands for Near Field Communications. Um…yeah.

Ok, so you know what Wi-Fi is. It gets you on the Internet at home or in the cafe, on your computer, laptop, or smartphone. And you know what Bluetooth is. That lets you use a keyboard with your tablet or earpiece with your phone. Well, this is even neater than that.

These are those "tap to pay" things. You know, where you just tap your credit card instead of swipe? Yeah, those.

Big deal right? Ooooh, like it's so hard to swipe that we have to just tap. Except… what if we tapped for something else? Oops. Got ahead of myself. Again. Stay with me here.

Those tappable credit cards have "smart tags" in them, kind of like the magnetic stripe only faster, more information, etc. So when you tap the credit card on the reader, the reader contacts the credit card company to see if the money is available, and if so, moves it from your account to the store's account.

When you open an email attachment, isn't it cool how the computer just somehow magically knows what to do? Or goes to the net to find the right program? And how your smartphone does the same thing? What about those quirky looking QR code thingies? Notice how your smartphone "reads" those and takes you to a website for more information?

Now imagine all of this at once. Tap your phone on a tag to open a file, including updated information from the web. Whoa!

At a museum, tap on the placard and the phone shows you the usual synopsis. But wait! See those links? Now you can find out more with a single tap on the screen. Have your headphones in? Well, now you can hear all about it, too. Ok, so that's cool and all, but so what?

How's about this: a nurse is doing rounds at the hospital, and is wearing a little thingie-boo on her belt. Every time she leans on a bed, it tells the hospital's computer she's there and reads the other equipment in the room to gather information about what she's doing. That sure would reduce the amount of scribbled, illegible notes, don't you think?

Or, are you a LARPer? The DM places the smart tags. Tap your device as you go through the game. Voila, it guides you!

Or how about a book? Tap this page to play the song the characters hear. Maybe shows a video clip or picture. Or some background history. Or the author's notes, kind of like the Director's Notes on enhanced DVDs.

This could easily be one of those life-changing technologies that we'll soon take for granted. Except for that privacy thing. But that's for another time. Seriously. Right now, YOU can buy smart tags for $1 each (or less) and start building your own uses for them. The only question remaining is... what would YOUR uses be?

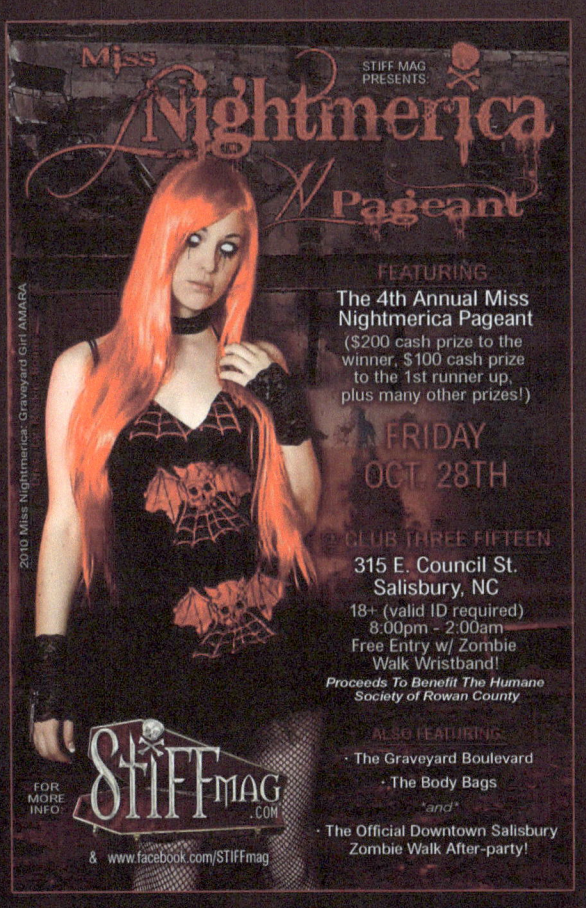
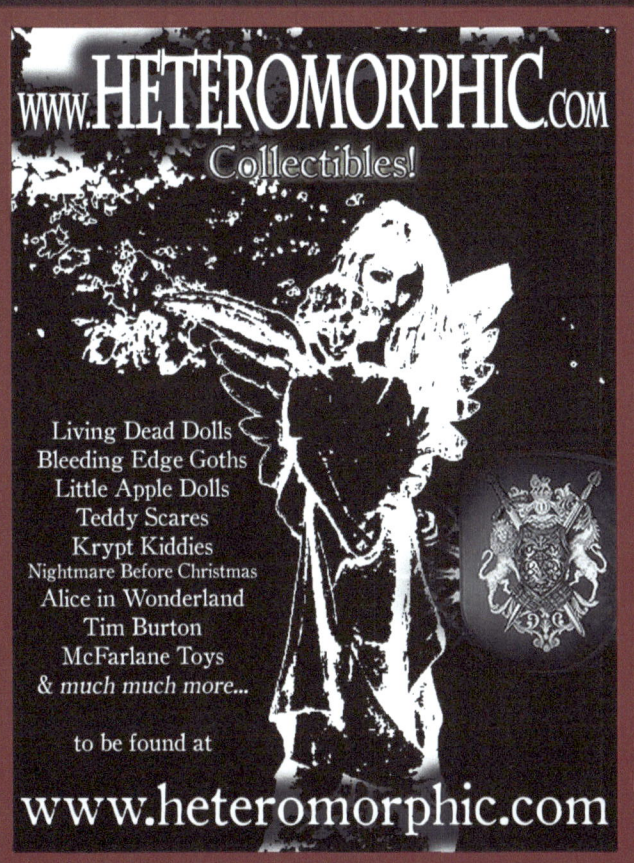

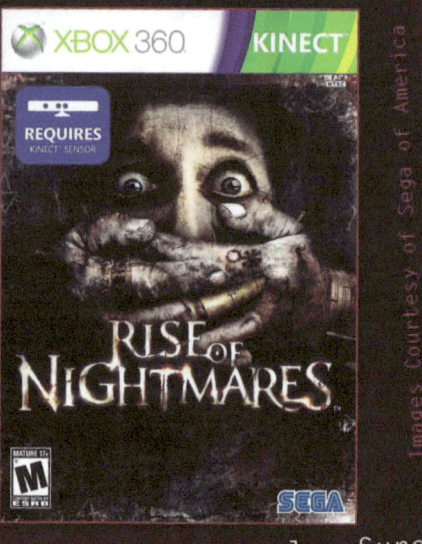

## "Rise of Nightmares" (Xbox 360 Kinect)

by: Dave Harlequin
(Xbox Live: DaveHarlequin3)

While it's no secret that I'm absolutely not a fan of the whole "motion gaming" trend, let me begin this review by stating that the main problem I have with "Rise of Nightmares" isn't the Kinect controls. Sure, it takes some getting used to, but I more-or-less got what I expected from them 75% of the time. I also didn't have a problem with the C-movie quality story or the unimpressive graphics because I usually enjoy bad survival-horror games. In fact, this zombie-filled, first-person brawler channels the weird vibes of Sega's legendary "House of the Dead" games more than anything else, which works for me too.

My beef with "Rise of Nightmares" is that it takes too long to figure itself out, and the game doesn't explore the horror theme nearly enough. Up until 'Act 4' I must have killed a hundred or so zombies using punches, kicks, and whatever weapons I could get my hands on. Most of the arsenal favors the melee end of the spectrum, and weapons break often, so a majority of the game boils down to fighting, surviving, and then searching for a new one before you're attacked again. As action-packed as some of what I just described seems, boredom seemingly sets in right away, and half of the time I just wanted to sit down.

In "Rise of Nightmares" players assume the role of Joshua, an alcoholic vacationing with his wife in Eastern Europe. While traveling on a train, a mysterious man kidnaps Joshua's wife Kate and the train derails. You find your way to a strange island castle filled with grotesque creatures, and the game unfolds form there. Movement is handled completely by the Kinect controller. Putting one foot forward has you walking while turning your shoulders turns your body. To fight, you assume a fighter's pose (think "put up your dukes"), and when you're not fighting or talking, you get called to dodge quickly to avoid traps on occasion. One of my favorite parts of the game forces you to stand perfectly still while a hulking (one-hit-kill) enemy walks by (kind of like the T-Rex scene in the film "Jurassic Park", with the general idea being not to move or you'll get spotted), and becomes one of the few tense moments in the entire game.

Around 'Act 5' is when the game finally starts to get interesting. At this point you discover the Azoth, a projectile weapon that uses your left hand for the rest of the game, and combat starts to be sort of fun. You can now choose to shoot enemies with a weapon that recharges itself instead of bludgeoning them all the time. It seems like a simple thing to get excited about, but I prefer this choice compared to walking around and only using one weapon at a time. Later, you'll get another projectile-based weapon for both hands, and the "House of the Dead" comparison becomes even more obvious thanks to the game's terrible plot.

Overall, "Rise of Nightmares" is average at best, and a shining example of a control scheme struggling to find its strengths in a full game. The developers purposely placed an auto-walk to help people who have trouble with the controls, yet this Band-Aid gets taken away from you in certain places, which forces you to adapt one way or the other. You'll spend a majority of the game fighting and swinging your fists at the air, probably looking foolish to boot. But there are surprises in this adventure... it just takes half the game before you'll get to them.

Basically, if you like motion gaming then it's totally worth a play-through... if not, then this is definitely not the title to change your mind. Either way, you can always play the "House of the Dead" games for around fifty cents at your local arcade... just sayin'.

2.5 out of 5 scars.

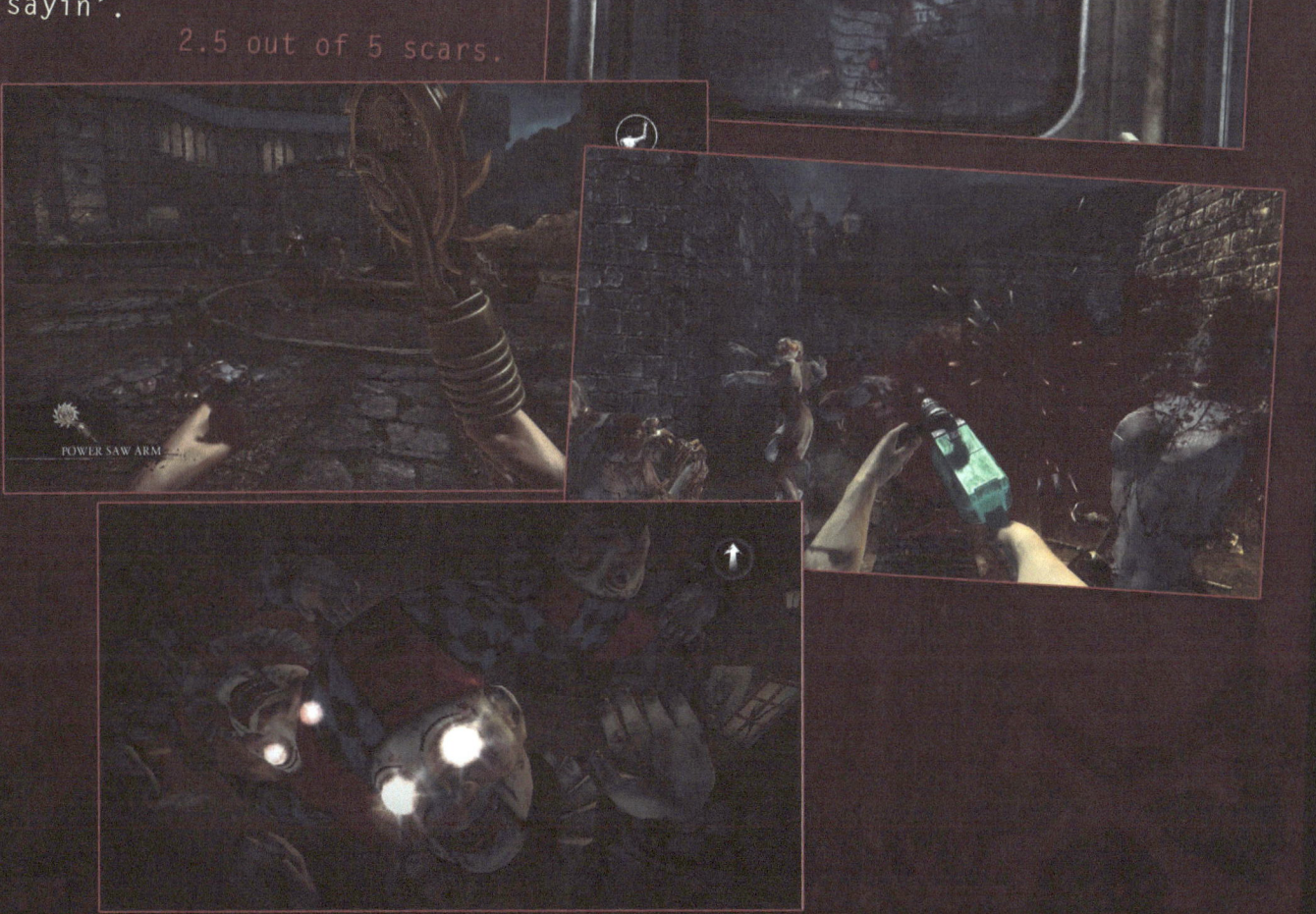

# UPCOMING EVENTS

STIFF

10/15-16: Rocktoberfest 2011: Enoree, SC

10/21-23: RoundCon 2011 @ Holiday Inn & Suites: Columbia, SC

10/28: 4th Annual Miss Nightmerica Pageant  @ 315 Club: Salisbury, NC

11/4: 2011 Fatality Ball @ Ground Zero: Spartanburg, SC

1/14: Asylum @ Juggling Gypsy: Wilmington, NC

2/17-19: Con Nooga 2012 @ Chattanooga Convention Center: Chattanooga, TN

More 2012 events to be announced soon. Please visit www.stiffmag.com for more information as it develops or to inquire about booking.

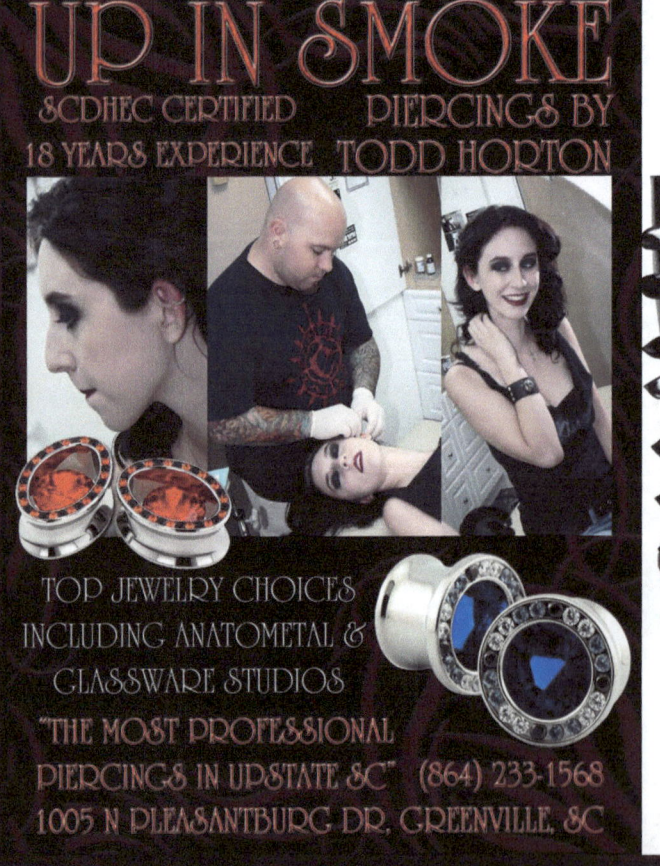
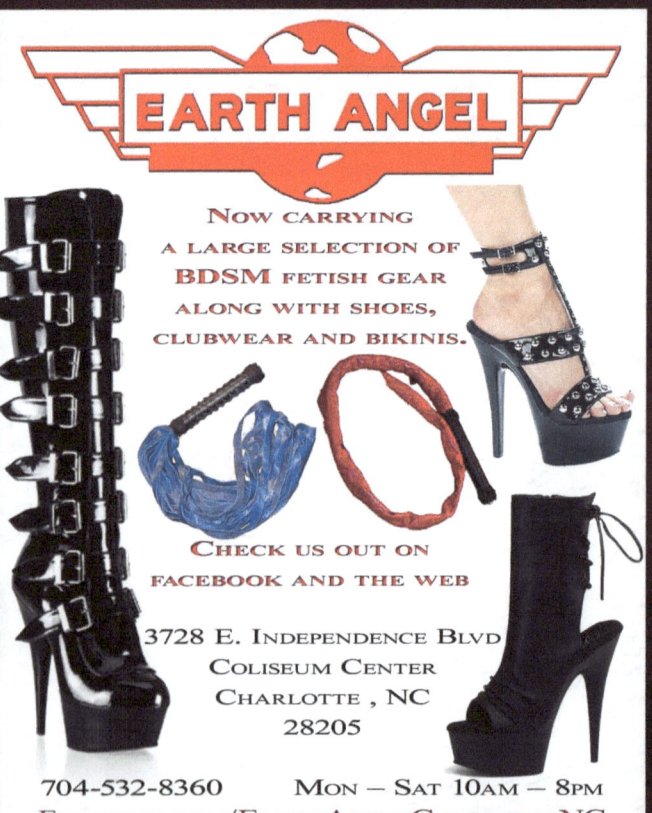